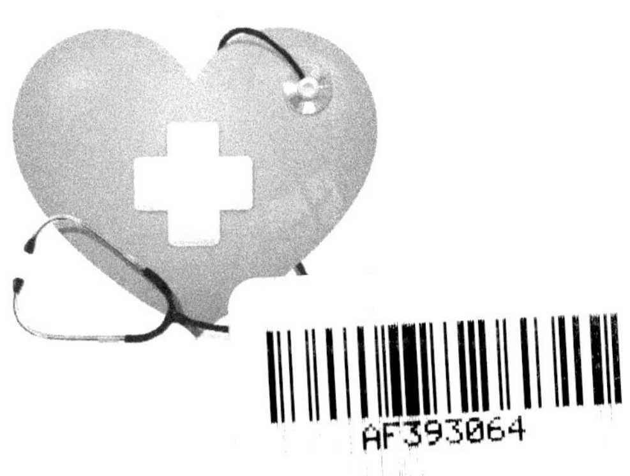

# IS THIS LOVE I AM FEELING?

## An Introduction to Love

*The Power of Love Series (Book One)*

TUNDE IDOWU-TAYLOR

Is This Love I am Feeling? An Introduction to Love
The Power of Love Series (Book One)

First Published in 2022
© Copyright 2022 - Tunde Idowu-Taylor

All rights reserved. This book may not be copied or reprinted for commercial gain or profit. The use of short quotations or occasional page copying for personal or group study is permitted and encouraged except for brief excerpts in magazines, articles, reviews, etc. Unless otherwise identified, Scripture quotations are from the King James Version of the Bible. The emphasis within Scripture quotation is the Author's own.

Tel: +234-80-356309589, +234-80-62655862
E-mail: tayloraflame@yahoo.com

ISBN: 978-978-50130-3-0

ISBN 978501303-0

9 789785 013030

Published by:

Road 49, Akin Adeola Way,
Lekki Scheme II, By Abraham Adesanya,
Lekki-Ajah, Lagos Nigeria.

9, Fatokun Street, Iju Railway Station,
Ifako/Ijaye LCDA, Agege, Lagos State, Nigeria
Published and printed in Nigeria and the USA
For Worldwide Distribution

# *Dedication*

*Oyinpreye, my Dove, my Undefiled*
*...with all my love*

# Contents

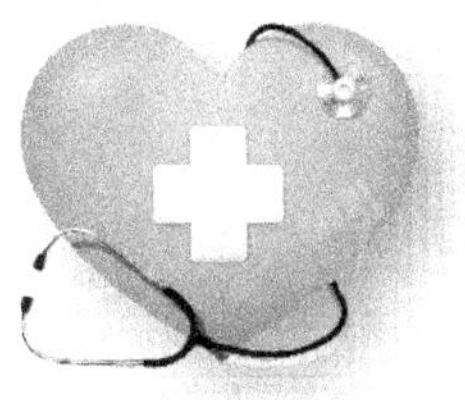

# *Acknowledgements*

It takes a man who has known a bit of love to write about love, yet, I have not arrived. I am a work in progress, like Paul, *I count not myself to have apprehended: but this one thing I do, forgetting those things which are behind, and reaching forth unto those things which are before, I press toward the mark for the prize of the high calling of God in Christ Jesus.* (Philippians 3:13-14). In my almost three decades of pressing towards the mark of God's high calling in Christ Jesus, I have encountered many loveless relationships, yet, I have also been graciously blessed to come across several men and women who have shown me love and affection, the way God intended it. Many of these have also directly or indirectly influenced my knowledge of love today. To them all I gratefully tender my unreserved appreciation. In like manner, worthy of note in recent times is Pastor Olajide David, Timothy Olaoluwa Bamgboye, Benjamin Abiodun, Ituazobe Eriaye, Emmanuel Ocheni, Ernest Igrhavwe, James Yeku, Eben Alonge, Brother Mike Araba and Onyeka Akaraiwe among others. *For God is not unrighteous to forget your work and labour of love, which ye have shewed toward his name, in that ye have ministered to the saints, and do minister.* (Hebrews 6:10)

Thank you!

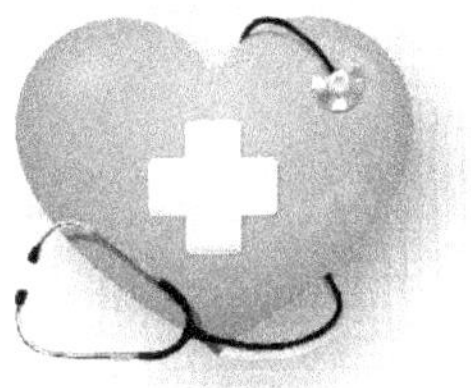

# Prologue

The world we live in today redefines things, especially the ones God has already given meaning to. Without a doubt, this is a generation that removes boundaries and takes out ancient landmarks (Proverbs 30:11-14). For ages, the world has been replacing God's definitions with its own and many have fallen and are falling victim to this misrepresentation to their hurt. In some cases, the misrepresentation comes with far-reaching consequences; in these instances, it will only take God's special grace for anyone to ever unearth the original intent of God. Love is one of such subjects. Someone actually openly said to me and the congregation at one of our conferences that 'love is a feeling you feel when you feel something you have never felt before towards a particular person.' That sounded more like a comic relief. I couldn't help but laugh it off.

For the secular world, the subject of love is such that evokes sentiment, passion, and silliness, and can be sometimes mesmerising. Many in the world conceive of love as a strong desire for the opposite sex and nothing more. In this case, love is reduced to the gratification of sexual desires. Some see love as a sort of sporting activity. To these, love is a game you can play with as many partners as possible. Here, it is not a big deal to fall in and out of love, to two-time their partners or keep multiple sex partners. These are the ladies' men or lover girls; they are the playboys and slay girls of this world. Predictably, this game doesn't always end well.

Yet, to some others, love is inexplicable, could be complicated and can be very confusing.

The secular world also sees love as giving, sharing or philanthropy. This is true to a good extent.

However, the Bible teaches that love goes farther and beyond giving gifts and sharing things, especially if the gifts are not shared with the right motive. Most of the world's philanthropists do so openly and most times to gain something else. For instance, oftentimes when politicians and charities give gifts, they do so with ulterior motives. Their charity is always a means to an end - an investment with a promotional flair. Yet, many see their acts as a show of love for their people. To men, he is showing love; but to God, he is using people. While men judge by sight, God judges the intents of the heart, not the outward act alone.

Most of what the world equates with love cannot stand the test of love when placed side by side true, pure, and genuine love.

Although the Bible is very clear on the subject of love and how to identify one when it shows up, it is becoming increasingly difficult for many to identify or test what true love is in their own individual lives and in the lives of many that profess love to them. There is a deceptive kind of love that proliferates in our world today. In the beginning, it looks good, glitters, and can be both attractive and enrapturing at the same time. It mesmerises, amuses, amazes, hypnotises and overwhelms for a while. It causes the heart to palpitate, defies common sense, blinds the eye, and could look very much like the real thing momentarily; however, in the blink of an eye, it turns into hatred, stirring anger, and results in betrayal and disappointment. This is what the word of God calls ...*a way that seemeth right unto a man, but the end thereof are the ways of death*. - Proverbs 16:25.

It is a pity that more and more, people are daily, carelessly walking into this adulterated kind of love because it comes with a sudden and overwhelming rush of adrenaline, is full of risks and adventure, can be thrilling and tantalizing, and is full of unrealistic/unrealisable promises and replete with sweet but empty talks (sweet nothings). It is like a cloud without water and comprises what we may safely refer to as pie-in-the-sky. It comes full of misleading prospects, offering promises of happiness, and security when in fact, it is risky, unsafe and dangerous. In the end, it leaves its victims sad, and distrustful; they feel robbed and humiliated. In short, they are left worse off. These are the unmistakable trademarks of puppy love!

When a person follows after the opposite sex blindly just because of a feeling that cannot be explained despite the clear handwriting on the wall that the journey is a calamitous adventure, puppy love is at work. When the laws of God are scoffed at, and good reason is suspended in the name of feelings; when unequal yoking, ignorance, the lust of the eyes, lust of the flesh and pride of life are the characteristic features of a so-called love relationship, it is safe to conclude with utmost finality that lust and not love is at play.

**Please note:**

The power of love is a four-part series; this is so because the subject of love is broad. This is Book one "Is This Love I Am Feeling? An Introduction to Love", Book Two titled "Love Ramifications", Three Many, Waters Cannot Quench Love and Book Four, "Becoming the

Ideal Spouse." My earnest prayer is that these books bring total freedom from ignorance, deception and confusion to everyone who reads them. May all who are in love also be released into the boundless ocean of God's true love.

.

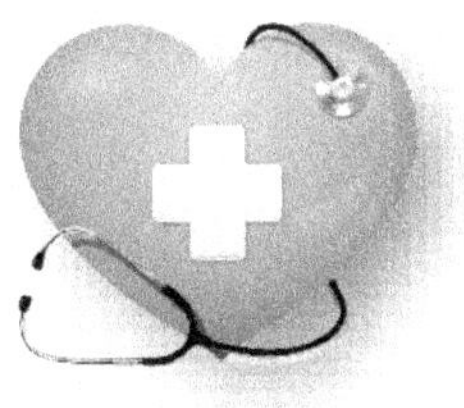



# PART ONE

# Understanding Love

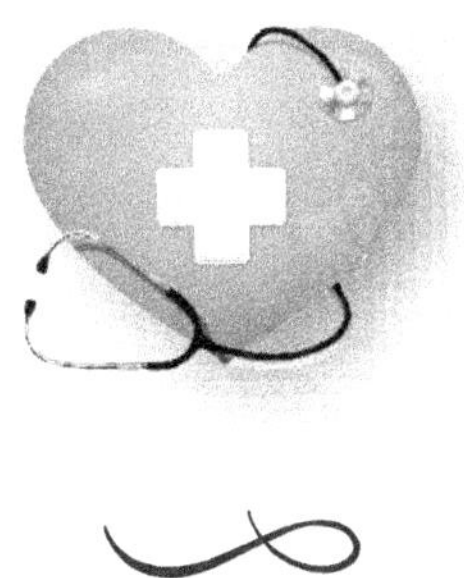

# CHAPTER ONE
## *Love Has Been Misinterpreted*

It is disturbing that our world makes so much noise about love, yet has no clue as to its true meaning, power and expression. "Love" is everywhere yet the "Power of Love" is conspicuously missing. It is equally sobering to know that uncountable books have been published with many more about to be published, millions of songs composed and are being sung daily, volumes of poems written and are being written daily, uncountable plays acted and are being acted daily, the world over in the name of "love" but when you take a closer look at what is being showcased, the opposite is what you see.

> There is an evil which I have seen under the sun, as an error which proceeds from the ruler: Folly is set in great dignity, and the rich sit in low place... (Ecclesiastes 10:5-6)

Most of what is being esteemed and portrayed as a display of love among men today is nothing but a display of lust - a gross misunderstanding, misinterpretation and misrepresentation of the subject of love. This should be of concern to every well-meaning individual, including you. Why? The answer is not farfetched. Every time people misunderstand, misinterpret, or misrepresent the truth on any crucial subject (such as love for instance), distortion of facts is what results, and the outcome could be disastrous. Generations yet unborn could even suffer and a whole generation could be wiped out as a result. That is why God in His mercy warns us in His word:

> Also, that the soul be without knowledge is not good; and he that hastens with his feet sins. The foolishness of man perverts his way. And his heart frets against the LORD. (Proverbs. 19: 2-3)

What Proverbs 19:2-3 quoted above implies is that the soul without the right knowledge of how things work is in bad shape; ignorance is darkness, and groping or walking about in darkness comes with grave implications. Consequently, ignorant people who are always in a hurry to get things done in their state of ignorance are prone to sinning or getting it wrong. In our case, people who merely assume they are in love without proper working knowledge of God's views on such a crucial subject as love and how it is meant to work will almost certainly get burnt. To bring this home, it takes a good understanding of the subject of love to get it right. The word "Love" goes far and beyond romantic feelings; it has ramifications that are far too great for the simple-hearted. Getting it wrong could result to a lifetime of pains and regrets.

## Comparing Notes

In the secular world, love is variously defined in different ways (you may want to consult some dictionaries). While many (if not most) of the definitions you will find have their place in the Bible, the direct opposite is what is obtainable most times concerning their application. It seems to me therefore that the world has our vocabulary but not our dictionary on this subject.

While it is okay to use dictionaries for purely secular academic purposes, it is dangerous for anyone to trustingly embrace any secular dictionary definition of some important subjects of life, including love as the true meaning or depiction of true love just because it is an accepted book of definitions, most times, these definitions are superficial and have been corrupted or watered down so much so that they no longer bear, communicate or convey the true intent of God. I'll explain why. Merriam Webster Dictionary for instance defines love as "unselfish loyal and benevolent concern for the good of another", as "the fatherly concern of God for humankind, brotherly concern for others, a person's adoration of God" (a most appropriate definition of love), on one hand, and as "affection and tenderness felt by lovers, an attraction based on sexual desire, attachment, devotion, or admiration, affection based on admiration, an amorous episode: love affair, the sexual embrace: copulation" (a gross generalisation of this topic which can mean the outright opposite of what is intended) on the other hand. If we choose to run with these definitions as believers, we would have embraced a mixture of truth and lies. We would have also reduced love to nothing but mere human feelings.

If we are to embrace Webster's definition of love in its entirety, then, what the scriptures describe as

- *inordinate affection,*
- *the lust of the eyes,*
- *lust of the flesh and*
- *pride of life* or *addictions, obsessions,*
- *fornication, adultery,*
- *lack of self-control,*

and other vices of the flesh and mind are all to be seen as love. We all know that this is not true. If you ask me, this kind of generalisation and misrepresentation has led to a lack of accurate understanding of what love truly is and consequently has resulted in several disasters that characterize today's so-called "love affairs" everywhere, including the ones projected in the media.

## The Media Can be Misleading

Without a shadow of a doubt, the media (television, radio, print media, new media, e.g., social media, etc.), have become powerful mediums used to educate, and influence nations today. Full-grown adults, young adults and children of all ages alike are being heavily influenced and controlled by these mediums like never before and most people are hardly aware of this. Superstars and other *influencers* of nations, including musicians, movie stars, on-air personalities, talk show hosts, podcasters, skit makers, athletes, politicians and policymakers wield tremendous influence through the media. Their impact on many is obvious and far-reaching.

Most times, much more than the impact of today's churches, the media's influence on families and family values is staggering, shaping and reshaping our tastes, lifestyles, cultures and worldviews. Obviously, it is becoming clearer by the day that to a good extent, today's media platforms exist primarily for mind control and profit and that, entertainment is a guaranteed money spinner for those who wield its powers in this generation. Most unregenerated users have discovered that youthful lusts, when packaged as entertainment, sell like nothing else; therefore, anyone with the proclivity and dexterity to properly package lusts and sugar-coat or present it as love almost instantly becomes the toast of the media and ultimately, of the modern world. Consequently, a multimillion-dollar industry of lies, misinformation, defilement, mind control and corruption has been built over the years and an unimaginable level of erosion and corruption of meaning is the final result.

Believe me, Hollywood, Nollywood, Bollywood and every other form of "wood" available today do not know true love. Instead, they have the wrong message: sex, sex and more sex. Fornication, drunkenness, recklessness, violence, rebellion, abortion, etc. Free and unregulated lewd acts on screen, pornography, homosexuality, infidelity, promotion of inordinate behaviours and so on. About all of what they appear to offer is shameful and unworthy to be equated with love. This is why most of these people projecting these distorted messages are confused individuals; many of whom are in bondage to diverse addictions, and need deliverance.

## Love Goes Beyond a
## Mere Attraction to The Opposite Sex

Feelings and attractions are natural and good, God made us with our feelings so, they are real, yet, they are not the yardstick to measure love. No matter how strongly one may feel towards someone else, the force of the attraction notwithstanding, it is totally wrong to conclude that what one feels at a particular time towards someone else qualifies to be named love. It could actually be nothing but lust, infatuation, temptation, or confusion. The feeling may also be borne out of a situation or condition which may change with time, after which the feeling itself changes. Feelings change, but true love does not. Love and feelings may look alike but the resemblance is nothing short of the resemblance of a house cat and a wild lion.

## Sex Is Not Love

Additionally, one of the first and most important things to set straight about love is that it is not the same as an amorous episode, sexual desire, or sexual intercourse. Yes, people indeed call sexual intercourse love-making; however, that is not true, especially in cases where the parties involved are not married couples. If sex equals love, then rapists could argue that their dastardly act of forced intercourse is love, while prostitutes would also pass for "love merchants". There is more to love than sex.

The fact that someone is all over you and is dying to get down with you is not a guarantee that he or she is actually in love with you. There is also more to sex than its pleasures depicted in movies and music videos. Sex is serious business. It is a joining of two independent people as one. Sex is meant to consummate marriage, it is for procreation, and not to entertain friends. "For this reason, sexual intercourse outside of marriage is not love-making; the opposite is true.

## Premarital/Extramarital
## Sex Has Dire Consequences

Sex is good in its right place but sex out of divine

confines has dire consequences, don't let a fickle feeling get the best of you. Contrary to what you see in the media where it is projected as being full of enjoyment and having no consequences, you could impregnate someone or get pregnant when you are not ripe for it; you could contract sexually transmitted infections; or worse, you could contract life-threatening diseases; you could even pick up a demon (ranging from unclean spirits of immorality, moodiness, depression, sadness, bondage to sin, etc.).

> What? know ye not that he which is joined
> to an harlot is one body? For two, saith he,
> shall be one flesh (1Corinthians 6:16).

Sadder even is the fact that many die prematurely because of unchecked passion. The Bible tells us that it is very possible to die before God's appointed time.

> Be not over much wicked, neither be thou
> foolish: why shouldest thou die before thy
> time? (Ecclesiastes 7:17)

I know people who died untimely because of the pleasure of sin they had for a moment. I know many who now constantly regret ever getting involved in a few minutes of premarital/extramarital sex. Visit the hospitals and maternity centres across the land and you will see underage girls die during labour or due to complications from pregnancies or sex-related issues. The media only profits from fleshly lusts but hides the consequences from the foolish. Be instructed!

## Evil Communications Corrupt Good Manners

> Be not deceived: evil communications corrupt good manners. (1 Corinthians 15:33)

The Bible is unequivocal about the fact that whatever communicates to or entertains humans has the capacity to shape their minds. Presently, Satan is working round the clock to see to it that he has maximum air time and can live rent-free in your head, all day long. Although many are oblivious of this truth but over the years, he has succeeded tremendously, indeed, lovers of pleasures are now far more than lovers of God and those having a form of godliness but denying the power thereof according to 1Timothy 3:5, are in the majority worldwide. How did Satan easily achieve this feat? Through the everyday means of communication, we all have grown to love and cannot do without. Evil information now freely circulates craftily buried in entertainment. Like never before, there are countless communicators of evil in this generation and the number keeps increasing by the minute. As a Christian, the onus is on you to know them, note them and avoid them; else, you will become corrupted, so easily. What you are about to read may not go down well with you, but it is the truth. Most of these secular songs about love are not truly about pure and true love. Instead, they are about lusts of the flesh and of the eyes; they are about *eros,* devoid of *agape;* they are like soup without salt. Hear me in clear terms, in actuality, sex outside of marriage is an expression of lust, not love. What most secular songs and music videos of today do is encourage young minds and the undiscerning on the part of immorality.

- They want you to believe that once you are dating or courting someone, you can go all the way to show your love.

- Worse still is the idea of one-night stands or friendship with "benefits". This is evil in God's sight and should not be encouraged among the young and old alike.

- They also try to popularize the practice of love, at first sight, the type that makes people go about breaking hearts, once they find anyone who seems to them like a better replacement. In this case, love is reduced to what you see and feel, and with no serious commitments outside of what is seen per time.

- Furthermore, these people are in the habit of encouraging, and popularising the practice of being in love with two women at the same time, (i.e., two-timing) which is the ultimate recipe for marital infidelity, relationship woes and family crisis.

Besides, most of today's secular songs play down the gravity of the evils of sexual immorality. They aver that any man or woman who is proficient at, and/or notorious for sleeping around, should not be seen as a prostitute who is dangerous to our collective destiny and whose lifestyle is all about the height of hatred but rather as one who is "talented" and "gifted."

Be informed; most of what the world refers to as love songs today are only deliberate attempts at popularizing rebellious practices and intentional disregard for the God of heaven as to where sexual activities should take place (i.e., within the confines of marriage). Sadly, but truly, they will continue to achieve their objectives without exerting much effort as long as men continue to give in to their deceit. If you are careless about this matter, you will be desensitised; you will be robbed!

In spite of the overwhelming evidence in the public space about the evils of misinformation coated in deceitful entertainment, it baffles me that rather than rejection, these people are well-received and rewarded for planting time bombs that can destroy the security, safety, sanity, blessing, unity, trust and peace that marriage and true love offer. This is the sad reality of the society we now live in. A new generation is being massively corrupted online and offline. It is now a jungle out there when it comes to sexual perversions. *And we know that we are of God, and whole world lies in wickedness. (1 John 5:19)*

Men are throwing caution to the winds and are turning their backs on the truth. Like no other time in history, corrupters and spoilers of our world, children and homes now command unprecedented following and adulation and those who should see to it that people are protected from exposure to corruption and obscenities are completely perplexed, overwhelmed, and unable to curtail the onslaught. Unfortunately, some of them are the actual sponsors of these corrupt practices, or what do we make of corporate bodies, multinationals, individuals and businesses massively investing their resources in spreading evil and corruption of young and old minds on cable TV, radio, magazines, newspapers, social media and other media for profit under the guise of promoting or celebrating love. Even the marriage institution is not spared as infidelity and divorce rates continue to skyrocket daily.

Sadly, but truly, a developing nation like Nigeria among others in Africa has continuously been weighed down by the incursion of Western powers, mismanagement and corruption and is already almost collapsing under the weight of decades of bad leadership and mismanagement. However, sexual perversions and destruction of family values being canvassed by liberals and other corrupt minds will not only weigh down the continent more heavily, it could outright destroy the entire continent like Sodom and Gomorrah.

> Righteousness exalts a nation: but sin is a reproach to any people. (Proverbs. 14:34)

> Therefore now amend your ways and your doings, and obey the voice of the LORD your God; and the LORD will relent concerning the evil that he has pronounced against you. (Jeremiah 26:13)

God's word is always constant and true, a national

celebration of sin cannot birth national greatness but decadence. When corrupting agents are celebrated as heroes, role models, career icons and superstars rather than a potent and ever-present threat to our wellbeing because of the enormity of the immoral venom they carry and are spreading all over the world at an alarming rate, like a deadly pandemic, they will destroy all on their path before they retire, if at all they too have not been consumed by their evil somewhere along the line. Don't become indifferent about what you are being fed daily, poison kills, even the strongest of men. Remember Samson!

> He that walketh with wise men shall be wise:
> but a companion of fools shall be destroyed.
> (Proverbs 13:20)

> Woe unto them that call evil good, and
> good evil; that put darkness for light, and
> light for darkness; that put bitter for sweet,
> and sweet for bitter! (Isaiah 5:20)

Any form of entertainment that corrupts the mind is evil. Love is not a reason for sinful and devilish behaviour. It is foolish to join sinners in pushing and furthering their evil inventions which they have wittily labelled entertainment. As a believer, you should have no hand in such malpractices, you should be able to easily discern good from evil and right from wrong, no matter how attractive the packaging looks. There is no wholesome life without wholesome entertainment.

For my people is foolish, they have not known me; they are sottish children, and they have none understanding: they are wise to do evil, but to do good they have no knowledge. (Jeremiah 4:22)

Sexual sins are grave before the Lord; don't let anyone deceive you into playing down on it. Again, remember Sodom and Gomorrah. Selah!

## The Condom Deception

During my compulsory National Youth Service orientation days, life essentials such as good food, clean water, good shelter, good toilets, etc., were not available. We had to ration everything and life was really hard. However, I was amazed that in the midst of the obvious scarcity of the most needed life essentials of those days, something was sadly made available in abundance – condoms. It was not only abundant; it was free for all and I could not help but wonder why. I later learned that it was being distributed by a nongovernmental organisation that was promoting 'safe sex' among young adults; they actually wanted us to practice safe sex while in a regimented camp. To the undiscerning, this was a laudable project, but to informed minds, this was evil, coated with good intentions.

I could not help but wonder why these people did not channel their resources into better and more pressing needs that we had on that camp; why they cared nothing about the precarious unhygienic living conditions we were confined to and how they could make it better for us; why the threat of death from hunger, thirst, lack of clean water, unprecedented exposure to mosquitoes, etc., did not bother them in any way but instead, they "cared" so much about our indulging in unbridled safe sex in our predicament. I also wondered why they took it for granted that having sex in the midst of the untold hardships we were subjected to despite the fact that we were mostly unmarried was our most pressing concern during our 3 weeks camping experience. I wondered why they did not appreciate the fact that as fresh graduates, we should have no business with indiscriminate sex, (protected or not), but be getting ready to face life and all the enormous challenges therein, particularly in a difficult clime like Nigeria. I wondered why they thought that the message of chastity was not better and more important than the free tool of immorality they wittily brought to the camp.

At a point, I stopped wondering because I remembered that we live in perilous times. I also realized that by implication, iniquity and the means of committing it will surely abound by the day, even in the midst of famine, wars, pestilence, hunger and untold human suffering (1Timothy 3:1, Matthew 24:12). In my meditation, I realised that the devil and his system (the system of the world) are always hypocritical.

How could one reconcile being told that the camp life was meant to be a regimented one (which means that we were supposed to live a focused, disciplined and controlled life in the midst of limited resources) on the one hand, with being also encouraged directly or indirectly with a tool of fornication (condoms), on the other hand?

Bottom line: the devil actually slipped in the idea of 'safe sex' among people who should be busy living a regimented life. Somehow, and astonishingly too, it was truly a successful idea as sexual activities skyrocketed immediately after condoms were shared. It became so terrible that the whole camp field was always littered with used condoms each morning and we had to clean it up before the day's training sessions. It got so bad that the camp commandant had to ban everyone from going to the fields at night. (Many years have passed since my one-year mandatory youth service; yet, till today, those who go for this service year still have the same horror stories of unimaginable levels of sexual immorality going on among fresh graduates). The devil continues to replicate this idea everywhere man is found on the face of the earth today. You must be aware of the devil's intent and strategy to defile you under the guise of "love", so that you can be on guard.

> Be sober, be vigilant; because your adversary the devil, as a roaring lion, walketh about, seeking whom he may devour: Whom resist stedfast in the faith, knowing that the same afflictions are accomplished in your brethren that are in

the world. (1 Peter 5:8-9)

## Safe Sex Exists Only in Marriage

Anyone who tells you to practice safe sex by using a condom if you are "in love" and must have sex is not telling you the truth. S/he is a deceiver. No sex is safe outside marriage, and God's judgement awaits all who practise this evil either on the screen under the pretext of entertainment or in on-screen movies or elsewhere under whatever guise. Colossians 3:5 and 6 read:

> Mortify therefore your members which are upon the earth; fornication, uncleanness, inordinate affection, evil desire, and covetousness, which is idolatry! For which things' sake the wrath of God comes on the children of disobedience!

As with all other sins, God is disapproving of fornication and adultery and those practising them under the guise of love may escape AIDS by having "protected sex" but none of them will escape God's judgment. This is aside from the fact that it has been abundantly proven that condoms are not the best protection from STIs and STDs; they are quite unreliable. The best protection against unwanted pregnancies, STIs and STDs which is 100% effective at all times is what is already clearly spelt out by our Maker in Colossians 3:5 and 6 above, *mortify therefore your members which are upon the earth; fornication, uncleanness, inordinate affection, evil desire...*

The best protection against heartbreaks and other emotional traumas resulting from *love gone wrong* or *lusts* and sexual misbehaviour is always and will always be God's prescription: ABSTINENCE! Keeping yourself unspotted from the world! James 1:27.

If you have been living in sexual sins, repent today! It is a lie that everyone is doing it, everyone is not doing it, God's children don't live in sexual sin. Stop looking to entertainers and false teachers for the correct meaning of love and how to practice it. Love and sex are not the same; worldly entertainers and mainstream media are only out to profit from your ignorance. Do not listen to them; nor follow their wayward example! Scripture says that you should "let them alone: they are blind leaders of the blind. And if the blind lead the blind, both shall fail into the ditch." (Matthew 15:14).

I'm sure you don't want to end up in the ditch.

## A Bad Tree
## Cannot Produce Good Fruits

Again, the consequences of misinformation and getting love wrong are visibly present with us today. Pause for a while and ask yourself the following questions. Why do people start up with a lot of sparks and fire and end up in divorce? Why the unwanted pregnancies and wilful abortions? Why do friends rape their own bosom friends? Why should someone keep hopping from one bed to another in the name of love? Why teenage pregnancies? Why the "motherless" and "fatherless" babies everywhere? Why is child molestation and abuse on the rise? Why are premarital sex, extramarital affairs, pornography, lesbianism, homosexuality, bestiality and the like on the increase, if all we sing about, talk about, read about in most books and see in most movies of today is true love? Without doubt, it is not, and the Scriptures cannot be broken, "A good tree cannot bring forth evil fruit, neither can a corrupt tree bring forth good fruit" (Matthew 7:18). Anyone who is not deceived or misinformed knows that the tree of love is a good tree; its fruits are also good fruits. Again, Proverbs 19:2-3 is instructive. You may want to read it again.

It is time to embrace the Biblical worldview on love. Are you ready?

# Important Precepts

1. Love has been misinterpreted.
2. Misinterpretation leads to misunderstanding, while misunderstanding or lack of understanding is the reason for abuse.
3. Dictionary definition of love is inadequate and can be mostly erroneous.
4. Today's media consciously or unconsciously aids this misinformation and creates confusion for the undiscerning.
5. Sex and love are mutually exclusive; they are not the same.
6. The condom way is not the Kingdom way. Safe sex only exists in marriage.
7. A bad tree cannot produce good fruits.

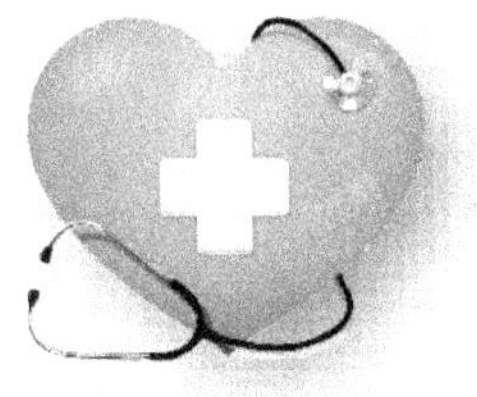

# CHAPTER TWO
## *By Strength*
## *Shall No Man Prevail*

Then he answered and spake unto me, saying, This is the word of the LORD unto Zerubbabel, saying, Not by might, nor by power, but by my spirit, saith the LORD of hosts. (Zechariah 4:6)

Yes, it is true that this chapter is titled, *by strength shall no man prevail*. However, do not get me wrong; love actually requires might, and in fact, is a function of strength. Yet, this strength is such that humans no longer possess due to the fall. One of our major limitations as fallen humans is that we are prone to weariness; we can break down, quit, get discouraged, be beaten down, and burn out. Many wonders why someone who once professed *"unconditional or undying love"* for them can just suddenly quit on them or even turn around to hate them. Many more are bewildered about the fact that the person they thought they could not live without at a point is no longer as bright and charming as they initially thought. The energy they thought will last forever has suddenly dissipated without remedy. Some who have been incredibly kind, gentle, harmless and loving at the beginning have suddenly become extremely unkind, violent and unloving. The same man/woman who was endlessly gushing over them has suddenly lost interest and is no longer wowed or charmed. Some are surprised to find themselves beating up the person they claim to love dearly, while others have actually gone on to murder the person they professed to love very dearly. Why?

There is a limit to which the arm of flesh can take a person before they break down on this journey; and trust me, most times people do break down irreparably. This explains why it is very possible for a man to be on fire today and become completely weary and discouraged tomorrow. Be not surprised my friend; there is a limit to how far the flesh, human will, emotion or intellect can sustain a man before he gets tired.

Stories of love gone wrong abound in our world today; you do not need to go too far to find several of such. So also, in the Bible, we read several times about stories of love gone wrong, even among the best of men. Take for instance, **David,** a man whom God loved to the extent that He actually boast him; calling him a man after His own heart - Psalm 89:20, Acts 13:22. The men of his day also saw his prowess early in life and spoke of him gloriously in 1Samuel 16:18. Yet, despite his rich CV, David failed in love and was almost practically destroyed by lust. He fell so badly into the depth of sin that one sin of adultery also led to another wicked sin of murder by this same man who was so highly esteemed by God and man - 2Samuel 11.

Just like David and ironically too, **Samson,** one of the most unusually anointed and unarguably the most physically powerful man that ever walked this earth was easily brought down by untamed emotions or lusts that he mistook for love. See Judges 13-16.

Why did these men and others like them fail despite their enormous potential for a clean record? The answer is simple; the best of men is still a  man and the arm of flesh will always fail a man every time, any day. …*by strength shall no man prevail.* (1 Samuel 2:9)

You may have been a victim of "love" gone sour or like **Amnon** in 2Samuel 13, you may have thought that you felt so much "love" for someone to the extent that you could not eat, drink or sleep. You may even have become *so vexed, that you fell sick for this sister or brother* until suddenly, the arm of flesh failed you, and like Amnon, *you hated him or her exceedingly; so that the hatred wherewith you hated him or her was greater than the love wherewith you had loved* *him or her.* In utter helplessness, unfortunate callousness and the worst state of depravation of your conscience, all you could say unto him or her, was "Arise, be gone!" The reason for this sudden breakdown or failure is simple: Love is empowered (divinely enabled); it is not by human power.

Regardless of how physically, intellectually or emotionally strong a person is, the arm of flesh will always fail in love. It is impossible for a man/woman born of a woman to successfully practice or live a life of love and carry on doing so without divine enablement. This may sound ridiculous but it explains why most "love" stories in the flesh don't always end well.

## The Verdict on The Flesh

> For I know that in me (that is, in my flesh,) dwelleth no good thing: for to will is present with me; but how to perform that which is good I find not. For the good that I would I do not: but the evil which I would not, that I do. Romans 7:18-19

After the fall, a verdict was reached on the flesh; a quality assurance test carried out revealed that the human heart and flesh can no longer live up to expectations The will is there but the power to do it is lacking,

> For I know that in me (that is, in my flesh,) dwelleth no good thing: for to will is present

with me; but how to perform that which is good I find not. (Romans 7:18)

The inevitable outcome is failure, falling short of God's glory. According to Psalm 73:26a *My flesh and my heart faileth…* To fail is to fall short, or to miss the mark. In sum, the verdict on man's flesh and heart is that they will always fail in their own self-efforts, especially on crucial life issues such as love. Mr Flesh cannot sustain a man for long not because a man does not will to love but rather, basically because he lacks the power to do so. In the words of F.B. Meyer, "We are not strong enough to win any victory. We are weak through the flesh. There is a leakage through which our good desires vanish, as water through a cracked vessel."

Without divine enablement, therefore, our will, intellect, mind or emotions put together are never strong enough nor reliable. They cannot effectively sustain the resolution, will or wish to love and be loved. This explains why any effort of love in the flesh will not always end well, and even when we truly mean well, …*by strength shall no man prevail.* 1 Samuel 2: 9.

In all, we must accept this truth as the unchanging word of God about man's love efforts in the flesh; it will always hold true because it is the creator's verdict, God said it, and our best bet is to believe it. …*Believe in the LORD your God, so shall ye be established; believe his prophets, so shall ye prosper (2Chronicles 20:20b). Sanctify them through thy truth: thy word is truth.* (John 17:17). By the help of

God's Spirit, the prophet Isaiah paints us the clearest picture of what's obtainable among men in their fallen state.

> The way of peace they know not; and there is no judgment in their goings: they have made them crooked paths: whosoever goeth therein shall not know peace Isaiah 59:8.

It is unhealthy to choose to pursue a love affair in this wicked state. It is even more suicidal to seek love from a person in this condition. This explains why most of our fairy tale love stories always end in disaster in real life today. No man can give what he doesn't have.

## Chapter Precepts

1.  Love is a function of strength or power.
2.  Human strength is however not adequate when it comes to the demands of love.
3.  This is so because of man's fallen nature.
4.  Even the best of men cannot sustain love with human strength.
5.  This explains the reason why man is unable to love and carry on loving unaided
6. Consequent upon this truth, only God's definition of love will suffice and our best bet is to believe Him.

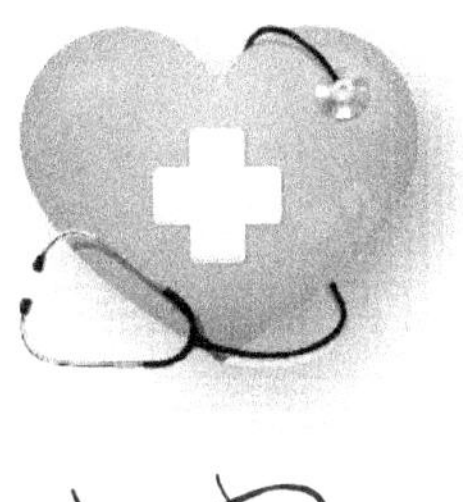

# CHAPTER THREE
## *God is Love*

As a direct result of the immutable truth stated in the previous chapter, (i.e., *constantly failing flesh and heart*), true love requires enablement - a type of grace that can only be received or supplied when man is reconnected to and stays connected to the true source of Love – God! This explains why the word of God concludes that of the many times when *My flesh and my heart faileth, <u>God is the strength of my heart,</u> and my portion for ever.* - Psalm 73:26a. Case closed! Why is this so important? It is important because true love is not found in man's emotions, or will; rather, it is solely rooted in the divine nature. Human strength is sure to fail somewhere along the line – it is unwise to argue with our Maker. This is why our understanding and definition of love cannot be founded on secular or worldly definitions.

In this chapter, we shall begin to explore the true biblical definition of love, and its implications. A number of simple but crucial foundational truths about the subject of love are embedded in John 4:7-8,16 which reads and I quote:

> Beloved, let us love one another: for love is of God; and every one that loveth is born of God, and knoweth God. He that loveth not knoweth not God; for God is love. And we have known and believed the love that God hath to us. God is love; and he that dwelleth in love dwelleth in God, and God in him. (1 John 4:7-8,16

These words are the master keys to unravelling the mysteries of love and we shall do well to examine them a little more closely as we progress on this journey. In the meantime, let's pay close heed to these important highlights.

## a.　　The Call to Love

- *Beloved, let us love one another*

Love is the most important duties of man on earth, but as earlier noted, in his present predicament, (i.e., *a state where man's flesh and my heart fails*), this call is a weighty demand. It may not sound as weighty until we realise how selfish the natural man is by nature. This is even made worse especially in these last days by perilous times where iniquity abounds and the love of many is expectedly constantly waxing cold, according to Matthew 24:12.

To love one another is the highest good on earth, love is the key to a peaceable, secure and prosperous life. The way of love is the way of sacrifice, forgiveness, healing, edification, prosperity and sustainable progress. Love is the key that unlocks potential, and the medicine that cures all social maladies. Love is the way to abundant life but sinful men do not know this noble way, most times, the opposite is what is obtainable among men because the sinful man is naturally wicked, depraved, destructive, territorial, jealous, and selfish. This explains why love is rarely found in politics, human justice systems or other institutions of men. True love proceeds only from its rightful source – God. To this end, Apostle John, knowing man's fallen and depraved state and having laid out God's demands, points us to the only true source of love – God

## GOD: The Motive, Means and Method of Love

### b.	The Source (Motive) of Love

- *for love is of God;*

As noted earlier, a fallen man cannot heed the call to love.

He is too selfish to love himself the way he should, let alone, others. This is so because a river disconnected from its source naturally dries up. The fallen man is disconnected from God. Consequently, his bowels of mercies have dried up, in this state, his conscience is seared as with a hot iron. He is a walking time bomb waiting to explode. According to Isaiah the Prophet,

> Their webs shall not become garments, neither shall they cover themselves with their works: their works are works of iniquity, and the act of violence is in their hands. Their feet run to evil, and they make haste to shed innocent blood: their thoughts are thoughts of iniquity; wasting and destruction are in their paths. The way of peace they know not; and there is no judgment in their goings: they have made them crooked paths: whosoever goeth therein shall not know peace. Therefore is judgment far from us, neither doth justice overtake us: we wait for light, but behold obscurity; for brightness, but we walk in darkness. We grope for the wall like the blind, and we grope as if we had no eyes: we stumble at noonday as in the night; we are in desolate places as dead men. We roar all like bears, and mourn sore like doves: we look for judgment, but there is none; for salvation, but it is far off from us. For our transgressions are multiplied before thee, and our sins testify against us: for our transgressions are with us; and as for our

iniquities, we know them; In transgressing and lying against the LORD, and departing away from our God, speaking oppression and revolt, conceiving and uttering from the heart words of falsehood. (Isaiah 59:6-13)

This is a vivid portrait of the fallen man's unfortunate state and what he gets when his desires or longings are separated or disconnected from God. Obviously, the main problem here is *departing away from God*. The inevitable outcome is love-loss. As it was in Noah's days, so it is, now. According to Genesis 6:5, "the wickedness of man was great in the earth, and that every imagination of the thoughts of his heart was only evil continually."

When Apostle John alluded to our next point of discussion, (i.e., the fact that: *every one that loveth is born of God, and knoweth God*), he was simply saying that God is love and it takes being reconnected to Him for anyone to be able to love the right way. You may have heard people say that God is love without truly understanding the import of what that means. First, *love is of God* actually means that love is from God, it can only proceed from God because it is God's exclusive preserve, He is the **Motive** behind true love. Mango fruit is the exclusive preserve of mango tree, for it is impossible for a banana tree, for instance, to produce mango fruit. Love is of God means love can only be got from God. He is the tree of love that produces the fruit of love. If mango fruit is derived from a mango tree, the tree itself is the mango because the fruit derives its name from the tree, as it is the offspring of the tree. Consequently, because love is derived from God, God Himself is Love personified, i.e., God's other name is Love. Love is His being, His nature and His person. Because love is His exclusive preserve, no other being, or deity can

    a.     be called love,

    b.     produce love

    c.     should be associated with love,

    d.     is able to give or express true love

In essence, without strong ties to the Almighty God, love is impossible. This is why I know that *Aphrodite* (the ancient Greek goddess of sexual love and beauty) is not love, but a mere *impersonator*. True Love proceeds from God alone and He reserves all rights and privileges to His belonging. He owns **the motive, the means** and **the method**. Man cannot correctly gain access to and make good use of God's exclusive attribute in violation of His *motive, means* and *method,* i.e., His enablement/power, definition, desire, intent, instruction or rules and regulations concerning love. This is why everyone without exception, who must love correctly must be **born of God** and then go on to also know God. It is safe therefore to conclude that God is the Source **(Motive)** of love

## c.    The Means of Love

- *every one that loveth is born of God,*

In simple terms, to be born of God is to be born again.

That speaks of reconciliation, restoration, redemption, and/or salvation, it means that a man has been reborn or reintroduced and reintegrated into the Kingdom of God and thereby, into fellowship with God.

> Jesus answered and said unto him, Verily, verily, I say unto thee, Except a man be born again, he cannot see the kingdom of God. (John 3:3)

Actually, Apostle John in this verse takes it for granted that this group of people (i.e., everyone that loves) are born of God, and are the offspring of God; and this is why they have the capacity to love in the first instance. *Except* depicts the only way without which the matter becomes impossible. It means there is no other way around it. Without being born of God, love or loving the right way is impossible. The crux of his message or teaching on love in the book of 1 John 4:7-8,16 is that, **GOD IS LOVE** and *everyone* that must love the right way **MUST** be **BORN OF GOD!**

# d.    The Way (Method) of Love

- *and knows God*

To know God goes beyond the ability to speak *Christianese;* it speaks of intimacy with God. It is to know God's attributes, nature and character. It is to know His words and His ways experientially. I know this because the word of God makes it clear that anyone who lacks the capacity to love is in that unfortunate state simply not only because *he is not* **born of God,** but also because he is *yet to* **know God.** Why is it important for a person to add knowing God to being born of God? The answer is not farfetched:

a.  It is possible for a child not to know his true father or mother. There are countless children across the world who have never met let alone know either or both of their parents. Such children will most likely be unaware of their parents' physical attributes, characteristics, origin and social status. S/he may not know if his mother is actually white or black (a white woman with a black husband may give birth to an offspring that may be a white, black or mixed race; there are also black couples who give birth to white babies). He may not also know if his parents are rich or poor, educated or illiterate, tall or short, religious or otherwise; he may be unaware of their likes and dislikes and the list goes on.

b.  Moreover, a person can claim to know God, when in actual fact he doesn't because his is a case of mistaken identity or mischief. Today, there are countless paternity disputes due to widespread marital infidelity. Someone could steal a baby at birth and the child may never get to meet his/her true birth parents. Thankfully, paternity tests (mostly DNA tests), have become the solution to such mistaken identity crisis and many have been able to find out, (although shocked and disappointed), that the person they thought was their father is actually not their true biological father. There are false apostle who lead men to false Christs and the deception can last a lifetime without divine intervention. God's paternity test for both cases (mistaken identity and mischief) is the fruit called "love". A person who lacks love, we are told, is not born of God neither does he know Him. Even when he continues to claim that God is his Father, a close examination of his character will reveal if he is right or wrong. Just as a mango fruit is not borne of a banana tree, once a person's character is tested against God's loving nature and is found wanting, we are warned to do away with needless sentiments; he is not born of God, and does not know God. The acid test of **being born of God** and **knowing God** we are told, is good works. Good works is not the outcome of a man's own efforts in the flesh; it is a direct outcome of knowing God.

> They **profess** that they know God; but in **works** they deny him, being <u>abominable, and disobedient</u>, and <u>unto every good work reprobate.</u> (Titus 1:16)

That's simple enough. A person who claims to know God will not be *abominable, and disobedient,* and <u>unto every good work</u> they won't be <u>reprobate.</u> Case closed!

c.  Interestingly, there are others who are actually born again but are refusing to do the needful in terms of growing up. Consequently, they are limited in their knowledge of God and may not be as productive as they should be in their walk with God.

> Now I say, That the heir, as long as he is a child, differeth nothing from a servant, though he be lord of all; But is under tutors and governors until the time appointed of the father. (Galatians 4:2)

These are *heirs* whose attitudes are not different from those of a servant. They have made themselves liabilities and if care is not taken, they will eventually slide back. A new convert who desires to walk in love must realise that he needs to pursue growth and be ready to make use of all of God's resources (Ephesians 6:10-16) that are freely made available to all who are born of Him. Babies cannot wield the power of sons. All who receive Him have however been given the power to *become* sons.

> But as many as received him, to them gave he power to become the sons of God, even to them that believe on his name: (John 1:12)

The provision is already there in abundance. The power made available to believers is the power to **BECOME** sons. It is a process and a journey, and the potential for growth is enormous and limitless. However, some are comfortable with being babies. Consequently, while being born of God is important, and is a prerequisite to attaining love, it is not sufficient or complete without knowing the Lord. We must *go on to know the Lord.*

> **Then shall we know,** *if* we follow on to
> know the LORD: his going forth is prepared
> as the morning; and he shall come unto us
> as the rain, as the latter and former rain unto
> the earth. (Hosea 6:3)

It is at this point that we can become masters; free from tutors and governors. This is where God wants us to grow to. It is at this stage that the time appointed of the Father according to Galatians 4:2 can be fulfilled.

> Now I say, That the heir, as long as he is a
> child, differeth nothing from a servant,
> though he be lord of all; But is under tutors
> and governors until the time appointed of
> the father. (Galatians 4:1-2)

According to Hosea 6:3, *Then shall we know,* i.e., the only time or stage in our journey of faith when we truly become knowledgeable enough to love appropriately is when we get to that stage or point of following on to **know the Lord.** This is similar to the idea contained in the book of Ephesians 4:13, *Till we all come in the unity of the faith, and of the knowledge of the Son of God, unto a perfect man, unto the measure of the stature of the fulness of Christ.* Until we grow into Christlikeness, we cannot become a people of Love. We may be religious and sanctimonious, but we still won't be Christ-like because we have failed to know God who alone is the true measure of love.

In Jeremiah 4:22, we are shown the outcome of not

knowing the Lord, even when there are good reasons to know Him:

> For my people is foolish, they have not known me; they are sottish children, and they have none understanding: they are wise to do evil, but to do good they have no knowledge. Jeremiah 4:22

The list includes
a.       foolishness,
b.       stupidity,
c.       lack of understanding,
d.       being crafty in evil doing, and
e.       not knowing how to do good.

What you do not have, you cannot give. This is one of the reasons why I know that until a person is
(a)     *born of God* and then,
(b)     *grow up* to
(c)     *know God,*

s/he won't be able to manifest God's most important attribute – Love. If s/he professes love, foolishness, stupidity, lack of understanding, craftiness in evil doing, and inability to do good is what would inevitably characterise his/her love.

In summary, two groups of men are here described in our text and his description is distinct. These are two men with two opposing lifestyles,

a. *everyone that loves is born of God and knoweth God* (referring to a group of people with the capability to love the right way because they have been re-connected to God or because they now share in this divine nature according to 2Peter 1:4).

b. *He that loveth not knoweth not God;* (referring to people who cannot love the right way due to the fact that they are yet to be born of God or know God.).

Immediately after these two classifications comes the core of his message, i.e., the reason why people possess love or hate – this is the fact that **...God is love.** A person is either of God or of the devil; we cannot have it both ways.

Conclusively, we are told here that love is not our feelings, our emotions, desires, or longings. Love goes beyond the "affection and tenderness felt by lovers, attraction based on sexual desire, attachment, devotion, or admiration, affection based on admiration, an amorous episode: love affair, the sexual embrace: copulation", etc.; instead, we are told that Love is a being, Love is a person and this person is none other than God. **God is Love!** He is the **motive, the means,** and **the** method of love.

Consequently, if it is love we seek, it is God we need. He is sufficient! His love does not fail like men's heart and men's flesh do - 1Corinthians 13:8.

Until a person comes to understand and embrace this

truth about the true meaning of love, s/he will always miss love. This is the summary of the idea expressed in 1 John 4:7-8, 16.

Loving correctly is contingent upon the fact that our definition of love is in tandem with that of Scripture. We must unreservedly embrace the truth that,

a.    *love is of God,*
b.    *every one that loves is born of God,* and
c.    *knows God intimately* because,
d.    *God is Love*

Anywhere true love is on display, this foundational truth is at work. This truth sets the prelude for all other explanations and exegesis that shall hereafter be made.

## Chapter Precepts

1. God is love.
2. Man's greatest challenge is the call to love others because he is by nature selfish.
3. Love is of God; He is the rightful owner of love. Love proceeds <u>only</u> from Him. God owns 100 percent patent rights to define and dispense love. He owns the motive, the means and the method of love.
4. Everyone who has the capacity to love is (a) born of God and (b) knows God
5. Being born of God is crucial, and knowing God (growing up or maturing in the faith) is even more important. Growth is essential; else, fruitlessness is inevitable
6. Claiming to be born of God is not enough; one must pass the paternity test of sonship through good works.
7. Anyone and everyone who is not born of God does not know God, and automatically lacks the capacity for love.

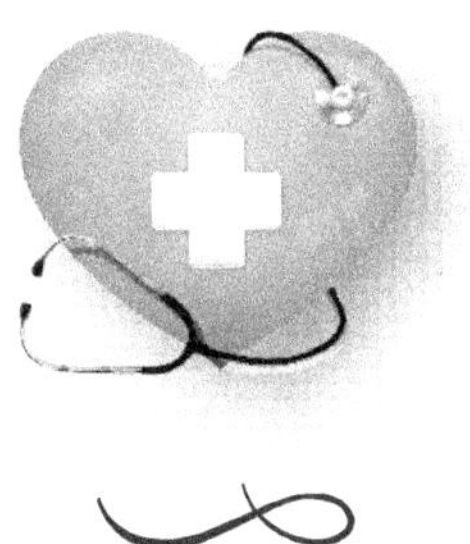



# *Love And God's Attributes - Power*

One of the ways we can easily see why love is God's exclusive preserve is through His intrinsic attributes, His nature and creation give credence to His loving nature and personality. Love is embedded in His attributes. Man is called to love, love requires power, but the power of love is not available in the fallen state. There is a need to access the source of power to generate love. This is where some of God's attributes come in since God's love is inherent in His attributes. To know love is to know God, and to know God is to be conversant with His intrinsic attributes, without which understanding and enjoying love and its powers are impossible. In the following chapters, we shall examine a few of these attributes.

## Attribute 1 - Power

Be reminded that we are talking about the Power of Love, and we have made it clear that love is a function of power, the kind that even the best of humans no longer possesses due to the fall. Most people who profess love are not oblivious of the fact that love is a function of power. This is why you hear them admit in defeat "I can't do this anymore", or "I am fed up or tired." Or "I don't love him/her anymore." At this crossroad, the energy to keep on fulfilling the requirements of love is drained. This is where even the most powerful men/women break down and shut down like a smartphone with an empty battery. Happily, this situation has a remedy. I have good news - the power needed for a lasting love life is available in God because power belongs to God; weakness is only found in man.

> God hath spoken once; twice have I heard this; that power belongeth unto God. (Psalms 62:11)

When the Word says that *power belongs to God,* it is simply referring to three things,

a.      God is sovereign
b.      God is able or capable
c.      God is the Creator and Sustainer of all things, including power channels or banks

- *God is sovereign*

First, He is *sovereign* because He is the supreme monarch of the whole universe. His authority is endless and all things are under His control. This is so because He owns the absolute right to do whatever *pleases* Him at all times and in all places. He is unquestionable!

- *God is able or capable*

Second, buried within His sovereignty is His limitless capability to do whatever He *pledges* to do. Being the creator of all things, His words are true, His power is for real and His pronouncements are law. He is absolutely reliable, dependable and trustworthy.

> God is not a man, that he should lie; neither the son of man, that he should repent: hath he said, and shall he not do it? or hath he spoken, and shall he not make it good? (Numbers 23:19)

> So shall my word be that goeth forth out of my mouth: it shall not return unto me void, but it shall accomplish that which I please, and it shall prosper in the thing whereto I sent it. (Isaiah 55:11)

Man lies a lot, that is one of his attributes in his fallen state, he is always trying to deceive others and he says things he knows are outrightly untrue. He is deceptive, cunning, and unreliable, as Jeremiah 17:9 puts it, *The heart is deceitful above all things, and desperately wicked: who can know it?* However, God does not lie, He says what He means, every word of His mouth is truthful and reliable because He is more than able to do what He says. This is why Hebrews 11:3 tells us that everything is *sustained by the word of His power*. He has ability and capability, He is all powerful, He is the Almighty. Nothing escapes God, He is dependable.

• *God is the Creator of all things, power channels inclusive*
Third, aside from God's sovereignty and capability, is what we may refer to as engineered power or created power banks or channels. These are the different raw forms of harnessed or harvested power in nature. All these are traceable to God. As the Creator of all things, God created and ordained man to work; however, work is literally impossible without energy or power. Consequently, man's God-ordained drive to find better ways to work the earth as ordained in Genesis 1:28, has led to many useful inventions or findings that aid his work, recreation, play and social life. For instance, man has found a way to locate potential power wherever it resides and put it to good use. Currently, there are at least ten known sources of power, which are: Solar Energy, Wind Energy, Geothermal Energy, Hydrogen Energy, Tidal Energy, Wave Energy, Hydroelectric Energy, Biomass Energy, Nuclear Energy, and Fossil Fuels.

## The Significance of Power

All these power forms, as we know them, are pivotal to a meaningful life, particularly in today's fast-paced, industrial, automobile, engine and gadget world. Without power, life and living will easily become crude, tough, rough, raw, cumbersome, and laidback. To a very large extent, everything depends on power. The post-modern man understands all too well the prime position power generation and deployment occupies in his daily life; so, he continues to devise new ways to generate, harness and deploy power for profitable uses. Today, life without power derived from engines, automobiles, aeroplanes, turbines, gas, water damns, electricity etc., is unimaginable. Power is life!

Good, disruptive and wonderful as these power forms are, they are all residual powers, and were created and stored up in their raw forms by God. This means that they'd always existed long before any man could discover them or tap into them. However, if care is not taken, the foolishness in man's heart could very easily lead him to arrogate all credits and attending accolades of these wonderful discoveries to sheer ingenuity of some super-brilliant scientists, researchers and inventors and forget their true source – God the Creator. Yes, we have the tendency to forget God or separate the Creator from His creation in the name of science. This is a costly error.

It is also needless because no objective scientist would separate scientific findings from the God of Creation. Consequently, the burden of reference is upon all scientists, researchers and inventors. The onus is on all never to forget the immutable truth that no scientist (no matter how highly intelligent) can create anything out of nothing. Only God can. Only God calls the things that are not (non-existent things) as though they were, or to existence. Only God spoke the universe into existence (Genesis 1:1-3). Therefore, every human invention and creation is traceable to God's raw material. Consequently, human *inventions* are nothing but *discoveries* of God's hidden secrets. Science in its entirety is therefore dependent on God, for this is the only logical explanation for research – the investigation, discovery and deployment of God's original works/creations for human advancement, development and benefits. They are nothing but fulfilment of Scripture – the scripture makes it clear that God has concealed some things and it is man's calling to find them out (or research them).

> It is the glory of God to conceal a thing: but
> the honour of kings is to search out a matter.
> (Proverbs 25:2)

In conclusion, all energy sources (latent or active), are traceable to God the Creator; man, only harnesses them. In fact, the very ability to harness them is also traceable to God who wired man for that task according to Genesis 1: 27-28.

Man has been given a divine duty to,

> ...Be fruitful, and multiply, and replenish
> the earth, and subdue it: and have
> dominion over the fish of the sea, and over

the fowl of the air, and over every living thing that moveth upon the earth. Genesis 1:28)

God is the maker of the constellations of the stars, moon, sun, waters, seas, wind, plants and vegetation. He is the one who trapped power in nature and empowered man to exploit it for developmental purposes. This is the reason why we must conclude that without God, there can be no life. He is the essence behind life; He started it all. He is the source of anything and everything we call energy today including the ones deployed for all forms of light. *In the beginning **GOD** created the heaven and the earth.* Genesis 1:1. If God trapped so much energy in nature so, much so that the whole world can actually generate enough electricity by tapping into nature, He can do the same to our weak minds and mortal body, He can power us up for love literally. Only God is able, if we let Him, He has enough power to channel to us so we can love the way we should.

## Power and the Parable of Electricity

Electricity is one of the primary by-products of harnessed energy. It is actually referred to as power. The chief reason why the word *power* is often substituted for the word *light* or electricity is because they both have similar attributes. God is love; power in all its forms belongs to Him, and one of the derivatives of His power is Light! This is like what we see with power generated in nature, it gives us artificial light (supplied through electric and solar bulbs and fluorescents) which powers our houses and allows us to see clearly at night. While the world is full of darkness, God's children who connects to His power grid are the light of the world, where. Recall that apostle Paul took it for granted that nature should actually teach us a thing or two about God and godliness. In the book of 1Corinthians11:14 he asks, *Doth not even nature itself teach you...?* This means that the God of nature, the Creator of what is seen, left some traces of Himself and what He is capable of in nature. His handwritings are conspicuously pasted upon all of His handworks. Nature is God's handywork, not man's. If we are objective, if we open our hearts and the eyes of our minds, we will see that God's glory is clearly revealed therein.

> To the chief Musician, A Psalm of David. The heavens declare the glory of God; and the firmament sheweth his handywork. Day unto day uttereth speech, and night unto night sheweth knowledge. There is no speech nor language, where their voice is not heard. Their line is gone out through all the earth, and their words to the end of the world. In them hath he set a tabernacle for the sun, (Psalms 19:1-4).

Electricity, for instance, can be gotten from the heavens, (solar power), by it we are able to power our engines, gadgets, automobiles, etc., it also provides light (through bulbs) dispelling darkness at night. So also, just as we can tap into sunlight and generate power, reconnecting to God is the proven scientific method needed to generate the much-needed power of love literally. The scripture is replete with this truth. Power belongs to God and wherever power is resident, light is never wanting. One of God's many attributes is the fact that He is also light.

## Chapter Precepts

1. Knowing God's attributes can help us to unlock the power of love
2. Power is one of God's intrinsic attributes
3. Power is significant for a meaningful life. It is a requirement for work and play, and is a sign of health and wellbeing.
4. Power or strength is a requirement for love.
5. All forms of power belong to God, i.e., He is Sovereign, He is Able and He is the Creator and rightful owner of all supernatural and artificial power sources.
6. Nature can teach us a lot about God's power and how it is meant to be harnessed in love
7. Electricity for instance can be gotten from the sun when harnessed and deployed for our daily power needs, so also, connecting to God and harnessing His powers is a requirement if we must wield or be able to deploy the power of love.
8. Since God is the source of all powers, it naturally follows that He is the proven scientific method needed to generate the much-needed power of love, literally.

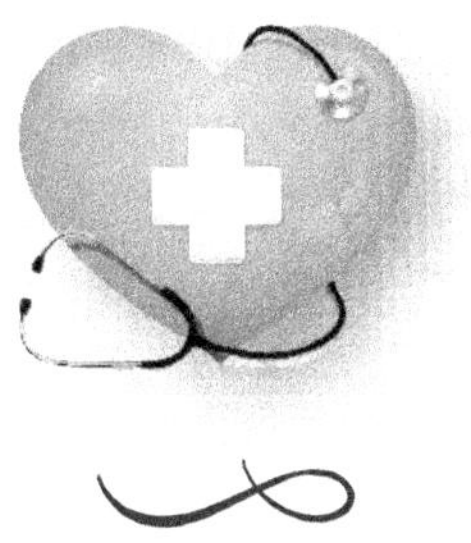

CHAPTER FIVE

*Love And God's Attributes - Light*

## God is Light

> This then is the message which we have heard of him, and declare unto you, that **God is light,** and in him is no darkness at all. (1 John 1:5)

Any time love, as a concept comes to mind, the idea or notion of light should also come to mind because another word for God is Light. Long before electricity from which artificial light is derived was discovered, the author of 1John was aware of the fact that God is Light and in Him there is no darkness at all. As we all know, there are different forms of light.,

    a. we have looked at *artificial light* gotten from electricity in the previous chapter,

    *b.* Light could refer to *daylight,*

    c. it could also mean *knowledge or intellectual light.*

    *d.* Closely related to (and almost inseparable from) intellectual light *is theological light*

All these are essential to our understanding of the person of God, and by direct extension, the concept of love and how it is designed to function in our day to say living.

## God: The Father of Lights

If God is love as the scriptures claim, then it naturally follows that everything else He is will also be love or an essential ingredient of love. We are told in the book of 1John 1:5, that *God is light* and *in Him there is no darkness at all,* but this is not all the Bible has to say about God and His attribute, light. James 1:17 makes it clear that He is the actual Father of Lights.

> Every good gift and every perfect gift is from above, and cometh down from **the Father of lights**, with whom is no variableness, neither shadow of turning. (James 1:17)

This means that He is the true source and author of light in all its uncorrupted forms. The first mention of light in scripture, was in reference to creation (Genesis 1:3) *And God said, Let there be light: and there was light.* It is common-sense knowledge that no one can give what he doesn't have. God commanded light to shine and displace the belligerent darkness that covered the face of the deep and it was immediately so because God Himself is the purveyor of light. According to John Blanchard, when the Bible says that God is the Father of lights, there are at least three lights implied.

1.  **Natural Light -** (Genesis 1:3) *And God said, Let there be light: and there was light.* (Psalms 19:1) *The heavens declare the glory of God; and the firmament sheweth his handywork.*

2.  **Intellectual Light -** (Daniel 2:19-22) *Then was the secret revealed unto Daniel in a night vision. Then Daniel blessed the God of heaven. Daniel answered and said, Blessed be the name of God for ever and ever: for wisdom and might are his: And he changeth the times and the seasons: he removeth kings, and setteth up kings: he giveth wisdom unto the wise, and knowledge to them that know understanding: He revealeth the deep and secret things: he knoweth what is in the darkness, and the light dwelleth with him.*

3.  **Theological Light.** This has double connotation.
    + The light from God's word that guides the believer's conduct and character - (Psalms 119:105) *Thy word is a lamp unto my feet, and a light unto my path.*
    + The revelation light that enables the unveiling,

understanding, appreciation and application of God's word through Divine enablement – *And he said, How can I, except some man should guide me? And he desired Philip that he would come up and sit with him* (Acts 8:31.) *But the natural man receiveth not the things of the Spirit of God: for they are foolishness unto him: neither can he know them, because they are spiritually discerned* (1Corinthians 2:14).[1]

Here again, light refers to
a. God's creation which enables the whole world to see clearly, work mor efficiently and walk around without stumbling.
b. God's knowledge of how creation is meant to function and be managed which He possesses and gives to all who ask of Him in truth and sincerity - James 1:5.
c. The knowledge of God which is granted in the Holy scriptures to guide the lifestyle of believers.
d. The ability to know what God is saying in the immediate or the secrets hidden in His instructions for a positive and fruitful existence on earth

## God's Dwelling Place – Light

1 Timothy 6:16 takes it even further, making it emphatically clear that God is not only the Father of

---

[1] John Blanchard, Not Hearers Only, Bible Studies in the Epistle of James - Volume 1, p.87, World Books London and Waco, Texas, U.S.A. 1971

lights, He actually dwells in light so bright, no mortal man can approach unto it.

> Who only hath immortality, dwelling in the light which no man can approach unto; whom no man hath seen, nor can see: to whom be honour and power everlasting. Amen. (1Timothy 6:16)

So far, we have seen that,
a.  God is love and
b.  He is also Light
c.  He is the Father of Lights and
d.  He dwells or lives in great light.
e.  He has immortality, so, He is eternal. By implication, His light is also everlasting.

## ✢ Natural Light

On several occasions, the Bible uses day or light to depict the new spiritual positioning of God's people, and night or darkness to depict that of the unsaved. This is so because when the day dawns, everyone sees clearly, darkness is removed and everything is glaring to everyone with functional sight.

> Jesus answered, Are there not twelve hours in the day? If any man walk in the day, he stumbleth not, because he seeth the light of this world. But if a man walk in the night, he stumbleth, because there is no

light in him. John_11:9

Jesus here uses *daylight* and *night* to explain the spiritual condition of two sets of people. He says that the one who walks during the day does not stumble, not because he is better than the one who walks at night and stumbles, what makes the difference is the environment where they chose to operate from. While walking in the *day* prevents stumbling, walking in the night (darkness) enables it. This is not all, note with special interest, that Jesus also pointed out that this *light* He depicts with *daylight* and the darkness He alluded to as *night* are both located or domiciled *inside* each of these two sets of people. This means that light and darkness are both situational. They represent the mental and spiritual condition or state of mind of these two categories of men. We can easily deduce from the Lord's illustration that the reason why many love stories are fraught with stumbling and inevitably injuries and fatalities is the environment or state of darkness where it is being practised. The moment a person steps into the light, his/her story changes from grim to hope, sadness to joy, hopelessness to hope and from stumbling to perfection.

## Light, The Atmosphere for True Love

To bring this home, God is love, and God is light, light is the opposite of darkness. To walk in darkness is to stumble but walking in light prevents stumbling. Daylight or light is therefore the true atmosphere or environment where love can thrive without stumbling.

A person who has light in him is a person who has true love in him, light is synonymous with the knowledge of God, it is akin to being a partaker of the divine nature, which is the guaranteed way to escape the corruption that is the world.

> Whereby are given unto us exceeding great and precious promises: that by these ye might be partakers of the divine nature, having escaped the corruption that is in the world through lust. (2 Peter 1:4)

Sharing in the divine nature is therefore an inevitable factor of love. Figuratively, daylight represents good while darkness speaks of evil. Most malpractices or evil take place in secret or in the dark. Evil doers and sinners most times, need the cover of darkness (for secrecy), to perpetrate their evil deeds. However, children of light have no business with evil deeds, the same way light and darkness cannot coexist.

> But have renounced the hidden things of dishonesty, not walking in craftiness, nor handling the word of God deceitfully; but by manifestation of the truth commending ourselves to every man's conscience in the sight of God. (2 Corinthians 4:2)

Note the word "in the sight of God". This means that children of light are positioned permanently in God's presence, i.e., in the light. Their acts are therefore influenced and engineered by light because they have been translated from the kingdom of darkness into the Kingdom of the dear Son. In God's presence, hide and seek, shameful practices or dirty dealings no longer fascinates because spiritual sight has been restored, consequently, people who have light in themselves live out their daily lives in all truth and sincerity, naturally beaming with love, and having boldness in the sight of God the Father of Lights.

> Giving thanks unto the Father, which hath made us meet to be partakers of the inheritance of the saints in light: Who hath delivered us from the **power of darkness,** and hath translated us into the kingdom of his dear Son: (Colossians 1:12-13)

Don't get tired of hearing this, true love is inherent in the Father; it is therefore an inheritance gotten from Him. Saints have no inheritance in darkness because God is not located there; rather, their inheritance is in the light because that is God's dwelling place. Consequently, a translation from darkness to light must occur before a person can become a person of love. The power of darkness must be defeated in a man's life before the Power of Love can become a reality.

Undue secrecy, is a red flag in love. True love solidly founded in God's power is expressed in all boldness, purity, truth and sincerity. Fear is never a factor any longer - *There is no fear in love; but perfect love casteth out fear:*

*because fear hath torment. He that feareth is not made perfect in love* - (1 John 4:18). Remember in God's light everything is glaring, there are no hiding places, no variableness nor shadow of turning. (2 Corinthians 4:2). When king David discovered this truth, he exclaimed, …*O LORD, thou hast searched me, and known me. Thou knowest my downsitting and mine uprising, thou understandest my thought afar off. Thou compassest my path and my lying down, and art acquainted with all my ways. For there is not a word in my tongue, but, lo, O LORD, thou knowest it altogether. Thou hast beset me behind and before, and laid thine hand upon me. Such knowledge is too wonderful for me; it is high, I cannot attain unto it. Whither shall I go from thy spirit? or whither shall I flee from thy presence? If I ascend up into heaven, thou art there: if I make my bed in hell, behold, thou art there. If I take the wings of the morning, and dwell in the uttermost parts of the sea; Even there shall thy hand lead me, and thy right hand shall hold me. If I say, Surely the darkness shall cover me; even the night shall be light about me. Yea, the darkness hideth not from thee; but the night shineth as the day: the darkness and the light are both alike to thee.* (Psalms 139:1-12)

Understanding this truth is indispensable to walking in love.

## The Indispensability of God's Light in Love

This means that the best atmosphere to seek for Love and the best state of mind or condition where love can be found is in the light. By implication, in true love, there should be no darkness, hidden agenda, lies, deceptions, or variableness at all. These are tough ideas for humans to accept but nonetheless true because they are the words of God. Believe the holy scriptures, if your experiences in love have been characterised by variableness (i.e., evil deeds, irregularities, abnormalities and/or indiscretion), otherwise akin to shadows and darkness, I can tell you for free, what you bear or have been offered you is not love but something else, you haven't found true love, because, as the scriptures say, *...in Him is no darkness at all.*

By now, you should have seen why all of the worldly descriptions of love cannot be embraced without any recourse to God. A sound biblical worldview on this matter is that true love and light are one and the same, light is the natural atmosphere for love and the two are inseparable. If power is truly available in love, then light will be the outcome. Love is synonymous to light and cannot thrive in darkness and craftiness. Secrecy, uncertainties, fears sinful practices (synonymous to darkness) and other clandestine traits and deeds disappear in an atmosphere of true love. This explains why light is what gives quality, credence and meaning to love. Light is the right sphere or environment where love thrives. Light is the fertile ground upon which true love must be planted, because it is the enabling environment within which love flourishes. Here is the equation:

> ➤ God is love,
> ➤ power belongs to God,
> ➤ power produces light and
> ➤ light enables and nourishes love.

By implication, whatever is done in the state of darkness (ignorance, secrecy, deception, lies), will not qualify as love. Avoid men and women who love and thrive in darkness and are crafty in evil deeds, see to it also that you are also free from these because just as plants need good soil, light and water to grow, thrive and bear good fruit, man's love efforts and motives can only thrive in an atmosphere of God's light.

So far, we can see that God is love. He owns every form of power, spiritual or physical, light is a product of power in the same way palm oil is gotten from palm cannel. Since God is also the purveyor of power and lives in the light, it therefore follows that light and love are inseparable. As a direct consequence of the truth, anyone who claims to have love will also,

a.  have God,
b.  walk in God's power, and
c.  in light, (intellectual light and theological light) radiating grace and truth and then, love as a result.

Being in love therefore must begin with being in God. A person of love does not only have God's power to back it up, s/he also has light, to guide his/her thoughts and actions on the path of love. A man/woman of love is a man equipped with light (and its relevant application), be it in the spiritual sense or, knowing how to appropriate what is known in the physical realm the way God intended it. To be in love is to be a person of light, shinning bright and radiant in this dark world, since Love is not an abstract concept but a tangible reality.

## Light and Love Are Tangible Realities

As we have seen, light in scripture has several connotations, but whatever form of light we may be referring to at any point, all derived from God Almighty who is Light personified, not only in the spiritual sense but also in the literal sense.

> And I saw no temple therein: for the Lord God Almighty and the Lamb are the temple of it. And the city had no need of the sun, neither of the moon, to shine in it: for the glory of God did lighten it, and the Lamb is the light thereof. (Revelation 21:22-23)

This city gets its light solely and literally from God's glory. Now take it to heart that this is a literal city, although it was revealed to John in a revelation. God's glory lights up this whole city, and it is so bright that the entire city has no need for the sun nor the moon.

*Chapter Five*

## Chapter Precepts

1. Any time love, as a concept comes to mind, light as a concept should also come to mind because another word for God is Light Power and light are synonymous.
2. Wherever power is generated, light can be available.
3. God is not only a God of power; He is a God of light too.
4. Light is a requirement of love. It is an essential ingredient of love and the sole environment where true love thrives.
5. God is the Father of Lights.
6. Being in love therefore must begin with being in God. A person of love does not only have God's power to back it up, s/he also has light, to guide his/her thoughts and actions on the path of love.

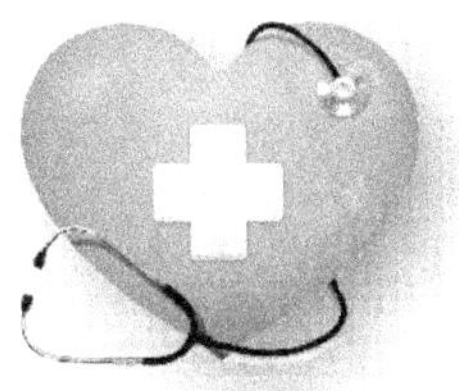

CHAPTER SIX

*Knowledge is Light*

Through wisdom is an house builded; and by understanding it is established: And by knowledge shall the chambers be filled with all precious and pleasant riches. A wise man is strong; yea, a man of knowledge increaseth strength. For by wise counsel thou shalt make thy war: and in multitude of counsellors there is safety.(Proverbs 24:3-4)

Remember, we just pointed out that light can refer to intellectual prowess. Knowledge is a similitude or derivative of light. Knowing how things work in the physical and spiritual is what is being touted in the common saying, *knowledge is light*. This simply refers to the ability to mentally comprehend a matter, and to apply, present or represent the same, logically. For instance, physical or tangible development is keenly tied to knowledge. No individual or nation can rise above their knowledge bank, for wisdom, is impossible without knowledge. Applied knowledge is what is known as wisdom. This is how man is divinely wired to solve his numerous everyday problems including the problem of shelter, clothing, feeding, health, and medicine, transportation and shelter, finance, power generation, mass communication and governance, etc. Wherever darkness prevails, ignorance reigns supreme. A nation run by ignorant men and women will always remain backwards until the status quo changes, the ignorant will always serve the wise of heart. This knowledge is also essential for interpersonal relationships. An ignorant entity will always become a liability to those he should be a blessing to. He will cause them troubles and set them back in more ways than one.

> He that troubleth his own house shall inherit the wind: and the fool shall be servant to the wise of heart. (Proverbs 11:29)

It should be clear to you by now that nothing thrives or reaches its full potential in ignorance, no, not even love. Wastages, frustrations, hardships and destruction are almost always certain when this is the case. An ignorant man of woman lacks the basic yet, essential knowledge of the art of living. He is lazy and laid back and therefore cannot give what is needed to cultivate and maintain the garden of love. In essence, he cannot replicate what is in the presence of the God on earth, because he does not know the path of life.

> Thou wilt shew me the path of life: in thy presence is fulness of joy; at thy right hand there are pleasures for evermore. (Psalms 16:11)

> Thou wilt shew me the path of life: in thy presence is fulness of joy; at thy right hand there are pleasures for evermore. (Psalms 16:11)

God rejects the ignorant, and needs His men to be knowledgeable.

> My people are destroyed for lack of knowledge: because thou hast rejected knowledge, I will also reject thee, that thou shalt be no priest to me: seeing thou hast forgotten the law of thy God, I will also forget thy children. As they were increased, so they sinned against me: therefore will I change their glory into shame. (Hosea 4:6-7)

The crux of this matter is that just like professionals are hired because of their knowhow, or knowledge. He also rejects men because of their ignorance. This is why He wants us to grow by acquiring knowledge. One of the fastest ways to become a person of light and love is to become informed, this way, we are able to contribute meaningfully to life and living, we become the solution and not the problem. No one gets paid for their ignorance, true riches come from knowledge and service. Living in perpetual ignorance is living a foolish life, because invariably, wherever ignorance reigns, poverty, darkness and destruction easily take over. The tangible presence of these ills is clear proof that light is absent. In such a setting, true love will also be conspicuously missing. Remember, *God is light and in Him, there is no darkness at all* -1 John 1:5. This is why light in form of knowledge is essential to getting love right. If all you have is your emotions, you cannot thrive in love because love requires knowledge. You must have experiential knowledge of how everything that makes life easy and liveable works. You can read more about this in book four (Becoming the Ideal Spouse). Yet, scientific knowledge is not enough and cannot stand alone because humans are generally selfish by nature.

## Knowledge (devoid of God's) Puffs Up

Academic, conventional or secular knowledge detached and separated from God easily derails those who acquire it because it easily leads to acts of darkness or sin. For instance, it could lead to pride. Remember, Proverbs 16:18 makes it clear that *Pride goeth before destruction, and an haughty spirit before a fall.* So, the important point to note here is that a person may actually be well informed and still be a person of darkness, especially when pride and not *love* nor a *holy reverential fear of God* the Creator, results from his/her exposure to conventional knowledge. Pride is the sure catalyst for destruction. While it is true that knowledge can be equated with light, be aware also, that a person may actually have mastery of secular every day issues and be devoid of the knowledge of God to keep him sane and humble. This is why a communist nation can also be one of the most productive nations on earth. We were made with the capacity to have intellectual (scientific) light especially as we continually interact and devote time and resources to examining and studying nature and other created things. We can do a lot with scientific knowledge however, against God's will and approval, what was originally engineered as a tool of love quickly turns to a tool of destruction. - *(Genesis 11:6) And the LORD said, Behold, the people is one, and they have all one language; and this they begin to do: and now nothing will be restrained from them, which they have imagined to do.* The moment a man turns away from Light, he stumbles in darkness - *(For the turning away of the simple shall slay them, and the prosperity of fools shall destroy them. Proverbs 1:32)*

The moment this happens, those involved set themselves against God and ultimately their hatred and rebellion against God is a clear sign that destruction is lurking around.

## God Resists the Proud

In actual fact, God fights or resists the proud but gives

grace to the humble according to James 4:6 and 1Peter 5:5. This means that love and pride are two parallel lines that cannot meet.

Pride is an enemy of true love; it is anti-love. This is why a person who takes glory in self, or in things but not in God will find it difficult to practice love, God's way. His/her pride naturally stands in the way of love until his shameful deeds are exposed and s/he is humiliated. We must acquire knowledge of how things work in the secular world. By this, I mean we must seek to know all we can know in as many fields of study as possible be they in the sciences, the arts, and other areas, however, we must never forget that the starting point or the foundation upon which our knowledge must be anchored is God, God is the moral compass of the just. To prevent derailing into rebellion, self-worship and ultimately, destruction, the fear of God must be at the very heart of our enquiries, knowledge acquisition and inventions.

## The Example of David

David is one of the classic examples of knowledge, skill and godliness, however, he so easily got into trouble when his heart strayed from God. In his right senses, David epitomises the balance of the knowledge a Christian should possess to be all that God wants him/her to be in love.

Then answered one of the servants, and

said, Behold, I have seen a son of Jesse the Bethlehemite, that is cunning in playing, and a mighty valiant man, and a man of war, and prudent in matters, and a comely person, and the LORD is with him. (1 Samuel 16:18)

David was skilful in all he set out to learn, he was a great shepherd, knowledgeable enough to defend the flock against marauding ravenous beasts. He also played the musical instruments of his choice with so much dexterity, so much so that when he played, demons relocate from wherever he was playing or departs from whoever he was ministering to – *And it came to pass, when the evil spirit from God was upon Saul, that David took an harp, and played with his hand: so Saul was refreshed, and was well, and the evil spirit departed from him.* (1 Samuel 16:23). He was also skilful at war, such that he never lost a battle. In the end, it was concluded that David had mighty courage and exuded great confidence. He was prudent in matters, which means he was a jack of many trades and a master of all. Howbeit, the moment David strayed from God's light, his earthly skills and wisdom put together could not save him, head knowledge failed him and in a brief spell of time, covetousness took over his heart. Adultery and murder were the immediate outcome - see 2Samuel 11. This explains why the scripture clearly warns,

Let no man say when he is tempted, I am tempted of God: for God cannot be tempted with evil, neither tempteth he any man: But every man is tempted, when he is drawn away of his own lust, and enticed. Then when lust hath conceived, it bringeth forth sin: and sin, when it is finished, bringeth forth death. (James 1:13-15)

David knew he was wrong by being with Uriah's wife, yet lust beclouded his sense of reasoning and impregnated his mind. He became momentarily proud by usurping his royal powers instead of submitting to God's sovereignty by doing the right thing. He quickly lost control and the rest is history. He became foolish and acted even more foolishly when he thought he could hide his sins from God. He needed God's great light to be beamed on His evil heart and personal pride to realise that God is light and nothing is hidden or can be hidden from Him. *Thou hast beset me behind and before, and laid thine hand upon me. Such knowledge is too wonderful for me; it is high, I cannot attain unto it. Whither shall I go from thy spirit? or whither shall I flee from thy presence? If I ascend up into heaven, thou art there: if I make my bed in hell, behold, thou art there. If I take the wings of the morning, and dwell in the uttermost parts of the sea; Even there shall thy hand lead me, and thy right hand shall hold me. If I say, Surely the darkness shall cover me; even the night shall be light about me. Yea, the darkness hideth not from thee; but the night shineth as the day: the darkness and the light are both alike to thee.* (Psalms 139:5-12)

Humility in scriptures is closely linked with a referential fear of God. It only comes when *God's hand* is upon a man, and when God hedges him in *behind and before*. The moment a man becomes puffed up against God, he loses control because he is not subject to God's instruction neither would he care to prove what is acceptable to the Lord according to Ephesians 5:10. The next natural thing to do in this state is to start having fellowship with the unfruitful works of darkness, instead of *reproofing them* - (Ephesians 5:11). Rebelling against God's authority by not acknowledging Him in all we do is the recipe for doing shameful things like what David did with the wife of Uriah and what Samson did with Delila that led to his easy capture by those he was ordained and empowered to subdue for Israel. Pride opens the door to shameful acts in all its forms. In this condition, shameful practices are but like mere recreation or sporting. This is the place where men begin to love shameful practices such as fornication, adultery, debauchery, lasciviousness, freethinking and all other disgraceful works of the flesh

> For it is a shame even to speak of those things which are done of them in secret. (Ephesians 5:12)

To bring this home, be aware that being knowledgeable is good and essential for love but being knowledgeable in several matters does not deter from falling short of what is right or derailing into pride and arrogancy and ultimately into awful acts of wickedness. For instance, merely knowing the law does not necessarily prevent a barrister at law nor a chief justice (if you please), from breaking the law or an accountant from stealing from the funds s/he is meant to protect and account for. Being an erudite professor of ethics, does not protect from unethical acts, guardians are known to have lusted after and shamelessly molest little girls in their care, meant to be protected, positively influenced, mentored and trained up for the betterment of the nation. The truth remains that in itself, secular knowledge, removed or separated from the knowledge of the Holy is dangerous; because it puffs up and can easily turn to foolishness – Paul puts it this way…*we know that we all have knowledge. Knowledge puffeth up, but charity edifieth.* (1 Corinthians 8:1).

## Chapter Precepts

1.  Knowledge is a similitude or derivative of light.
2.  The knowledge of how things work (Intellectual knowledge), is essential in love because it is about solving problems, it is the key to a productive and meaningful existence on earth.
3.  However, intellectual knowledge can easily lead to pride, rebellion and ultimately destruction especially when detached from God, the father of lights

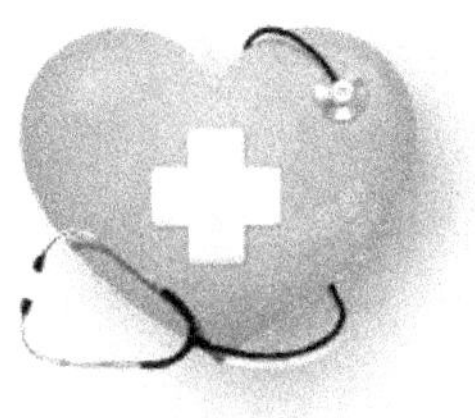

# CHAPTER SEVEN
## *True Light (Knowledge)*
## *Begins with A Divine Encounter*

As we have seen in the previous chapter, knowledge of how things work is good and essential and is meant to build up, edify or solve problems but devoid of the fear of God, the opposite is what will be obtainable. This explains why people use their exalted positions of authority attained through many years of study, training and practice to exploit the weak, rob the ignorant and proudly dispossess others of their valuables. It is through knowledge of how to make advanced assault rifles, chains and ships and use them skilfully that the Portuguese and the West were able to capture many Africans, callously separating them from their family and loved ones. Once captured through superior firepower, what followed was to be forcefully chained like animals and led into lifelong slavery against their own wishes. Sadly, many who resisted were not only mercilessly punished as some were brutalised, maimed or killed. Without a shadow of a doubt, knowledge separated from and applied without the fear of God is the reason for many of humanity's woes. There is no limit to the evil unregenerated mortal man is capable of through knowledge not anchored on the fear of God.

## Evil Acts Motivated by the Knowledge of Good

Ironically, most evil deeds are mostly motivated by *lust* or the desire for *a good life*, a desire to possess wealth and to be a person of means, a desire for power or to be in charge, a desire for gains and not to suffer hunger or loss. This is the by-product of the knowledge of good and evil which leads men to rob, rape, cheat, maim and when necessary, kill others so as not to be robbed, raped, cheated, maimed or killed.

This is called the survival of the fittest. In the bid to become rich and affluent, a man freely uses his knowledge to dispossess his fellow men of their hard-earned position, goods or valuables. He wouldn't stop there but will go as far as dispossessing those he could of their God-given freedoms. Deploying knowledge and great invention (devoid of godliness), he would go to any length (even the extent of displacing, maiming or killing his fellow men) just to achieve his dream of a "good life".

A classic example of this is the sad story of a man who fell among robbers somewhere around my estate on Lagos Island. As I write this, it is barely 24 hours that some young men through covetousness chartered this innocent man's tricycle for a fee. Unfortunately, when they got to a deserted part of the estate where he was to drop them off, they killed him with a mortar pistol and threw his lifeless body out of the tricycle and made away with his vehicle. This dastardly act was most likely motivated by the recent high demand for tricycles among tricycle riders due to the ban on motorcycles popularly called Okada by the Lagos state government.

Apparently, this man was dispossessed of his belonging after being mindlessly murdered so that someone or a group of persons can possess, own or sell a tricycle for personal gains. Those who took his life did not think of his desire to live, his family who are dependent on him, (including maybe aged parents, siblings, wife and children). All they cared about was their own immediate need for good stuff like immediate financial, material or social gains. In their bid to live, they took the life of another, the desire for money or prestige drove them to murder and robbery. Such is the power of the knowledge of good and evil, such is the extent of evil possible with those who *love* to have things and would exploit any **<u>known</u>** or possible means of acquiring it.

> For the love of money is the root of all evil:
> which while some coveted after, they have
> erred from the faith, and pierced themselves
> through with many sorrows. (1 Timothy
> 6:10)

This is what is always obtainable with a godless mind who professes love. Everything must be manipulated and bent to his selfish whims and caprices. Be wary of wicked men and women who come to you with a pretentious love they've never experienced nor possess. The Bible speaks of one of the major markers of the last days. There will be many inventors of evil things – See Romans 1:30.

We all know that it takes knowledge to be an inventor, but instead of inventing good things, many of our last days' inventors will rather invent evil things primarily because the supposed light in them is actually darkness.

> But if thine eye be evil, thy whole body shall
> be full of darkness. <u>If therefore the light that
> is in thee be darkness,</u> how great is that
> darkness! (Matthew 6:23)

Somewhere in the cover of darkness, an inventor of evil things whose mind could only conceive of murder when thinking of the easiest way to have a tricycle would be rejoicing for succeeding at acquiring one by murder, he could also throw a party and be congratulated, he could also win the heart of a love interest by showing off his newest acquisition but God sees him and like Cain who killed his brother Abel, his blood will be required of him. For this cause, you must be careful to know the true character of the person showing interest in you romantically or the kind of company you keep. He/she may only be interested in your possessions, beauty or accolades and the moment s/he is able to lay hands on the much-desired price, you become easily dispensable. Many have lost their lives this way. Be careful out there, evil abounds! A natural man can take a good look at a successful or knowledgeable person and his/her accomplishments and be so impressed to the extent of exclaiming – wao! But God could be seeing the same man differently, pronouncing woes!

> Backbiters, haters of God, despiteful, proud, boasters, inventors of evil things, disobedient to parents, (Romans 1:30)

The only condition needed for a person to become all these listed in Romans 1:30 and much more, is to reject the knowledge and sovereignty of God, walking about with carnal knowledge of perceived good and evil. This explains why the saying, "knowledge is light", is a half-truth. Half-truth is not truth at all. The right way to say it: is like this: "the knowledge of the holy (God) is light" – Proverbs 9:10 says it better.

> The fear of the LORD is the beginning of wisdom: and the knowledge of the holy is

understanding. (Proverbs 9:10)

As noted earlier, everyone and anyone can show affection and will show it at one point or the other. Everyone will profess love but the power to do it right only comes from the knowledge (light) of the Holy One of Israel. Anyone who hasn't encountered God's light may show "genuine" affection but will lack the power and the requisite know-how to apply, sustain or manage such genuine affection the right way. This is so because although s/he may be generally adjudged as a great person of knowledge, as an academic juggernaut, or a colossus in his/her chosen career, yet, if God is not His/her Lord and Saviour, s/he is not only in darkness, s/he is darkness personified. That sounds harsh but is the bitter truth. We were all in this state at some point, according to Ephesians 5:8.

> For ye were sometimes darkness, but now are ye light in the Lord: walk as children of light: (Ephesians 5:8)

Consequently, his/her understanding of how love should work is also darkened. This explains why the light of our love must be kindled by the knowledge of God. We must not only encounter God's light, we must dwell in it and ultimately become one with light. Love or affection gotten from a fallen man's emotions, passion or wisdom is running on a borrowed time, secular or conventional relationship wisdom will not endure. Without the knowledge of the Holy One, corruption, deceit, lies, exploitations, and brute wickedness naturally take the place of loving kindness, a personality whose positioning and habitat is darkness cannot radiate the light and love of God. This is so because God does not only dwell in light, He is the Father of lights.

Greed and wickedness are rooted in the heart and are never cured by secular or academic prowess or light, it takes a serious encounter with the Holy one of Israel to know, embrace and practice the reverential fear of God. Once the fear of God is not in the heart of the person offering you love, unimaginable evil disguised as good, walking on two legs is what is being. Without an encounter with the transforming light from God's presence, a natural or merely religious man is like Saul before he became Paul, s/he is *a blasphemer, and a persecutor, and injurious*: s/he is *ignorant* and full of *unbelief.* This is a rule of thumb even among those who claim to be moralists because what is seen with the natural eyes easily lures, tempts and traps those who look upon them with a carnal mind. Morality is impossible without the God of truth who alone is the source, standard and means of true morality. *But the natural man receiveth not the things of the Spirit of God: for they are foolishness unto him: neither can he know them, because they are spiritually discerned.* (1 Corinthians 2:14)

## The Example of Saul

It should interest you that the same Saul, who was once high on religious and conventional knowledge and was a proud *moralist*, boasting in his secular and religious knowledge, affiliation and achievements as seen in the book of Philippians 3, quoted below:

> Though I might also have confidence in the flesh. If any other man thinketh that he hath whereof he might trust in the flesh, I more: Circumcised the eighth day, of the stock of Israel, of the tribe of Benjamin, an Hebrew of the Hebrews; as touching the law, a Pharisee; Concerning zeal, persecuting the church; touching the righteousness which is in the law, blameless. Philippians 3:4-6,

He was all these *wonderful things* and yet remained a *blasphemer, and a persecutor, and injurious* man full of *ignorance and unbelief* until the day he encountered the true transforming light from God's throne. Apparently, all these years before his encounter, Saul was a self-righteous <u>literate illiterate,</u> until God had mercy on him and allowed him a glimpse into the true light.

> And it came to pass, that, as I made my journey, and was come nigh unto Damascus about noon, suddenly there shone **from heaven** a **great light** round about me. And I fell unto the ground, and heard a voice saying unto me, Saul, Saul, why persecutest thou me? And I answered, Who art thou, Lord? And he said unto me, I am Jesus of

Nazareth, whom thou persecutest. And they that were with me saw indeed **the ligh**t, and **were afraid**; but they heard not the voice of him that spake to me. And I said, What shall I do, Lord? And the Lord said unto me, Arise, and go into Damascus; and there it shall be told thee of all things which are appointed for thee to do. And when **I could not see** for **the glory of that light,** being led by the hand of them that were with me, I came into Damascus. (Acts 22:6-11)

Now, pay close attention to these words -
a. **from heaven**
b. a **great light**

Admittedly. the wisdom and knowledge of men have led to many wonderful advances for humanity, while God is the author of this earthly wisdom in man, at the fall it was corrupted. As it is today, it all lacks the power to transform the greatest of men because man is earthly and his knowledge can be easily compromised. For this reason, many have used and continue to use their knowledge to deceive, enslave, exploit, extort, defile and even destroy others, *But the wisdom that is <u>from above</u> is first pure, then peaceable, gentle, and easy to be intreated, full of mercy and good fruits, without partiality, and without hypocrisy.* (James 3:17). This is why it is not just a light but a great light. The wisdom from above is far greater than our *sense knowledge,* it goes beyond our mental calculations and permutations, it is overwhelming, transforming and humbling at the same time.

Unfortunately, the world does not possess this kind of wisdom, in fact, through wisdom, the world has turned its back on God, this is the ill-fated position where the world stands today – the dangerous threshold of atheism where modern-day science and scientists are made to assume that there is no God or to persecute God, or be injurious to their fellow humans like Saul was, or to aver that the knowledge acquired through science or scientific findings is superior to the knowledge of God. The Bible calls this foolishness caused by an evil heart of unbelief which results in rejecting God and anything godly.

> For after that in the wisdom of God the world by wisdom knew not God, it pleased God by the foolishness of preaching to save them that believe. (1 Corinthians 1:21)

Let me be very clear, anywhere men covertly or overtly reject God and His words, love vanishes, darkness quickly engulfs such a place and wickedness inevitably reigns supreme. Dangerous human and animal experiments will also result because truth will become relative and permissiveness will be the law of life. Godly fear and ethics will be replaced by chemical and situational truths. Nothing will be altruistic and nothing will be right or wrong. In this state, the extent of wickedness possible is unimaginable. Any society where this is the case will be rife with lack of truth, and absence of commitment or dedication to godly causes. Ultimately wicked devices will give rise to a mindless and godless generation that sees nothing wrong with the works of the flesh.

> Now the works of the flesh are manifest, which are these; Adultery, fornication, uncleanness, lasciviousness, Idolatry, witchcraft, hatred, variance, emulations, wrath, strife, seditions, heresies, Envyings, murders, drunkenness, revellings, and such like... (Galatians 5:19)

Do not make yourself the Petri dish is someone else's experiment. We all know that all these listed above only lead to more and more ungodliness. Adultery has the capacity to break marriages, fornication leads to unwanted pregnancies, which can also lead to wilful abortion or killing of the unborn which is a form of murder. Diseases and pains can also result from all of these wicked practices which are often wrongly hinged upon love as the motivator when in actual fact, the opposite is the truth. Now note that verse 19 states it categorically - *of the which I tell you before, as I have also told you in time past, that they which do such things <u>shall not inherit the kingdom of God.</u>*

No one knows the HOLY and continues to enjoy his/her unholy alliances and lifestyle. Sin sinks sinners because the wages of sin is death – Romans 6:23. Take this truth very seriously, knowledge (of the sciences, crafts and the arts) disconnected from God will always result in calamities, just as …*the turning away of the simple shall slay them, and the prosperity of fools shall destroy them..* (Proverbs 1:32). If this truth is not made plain immediately, it will ultimately come to the fore someday in the near future. It takes an evil heart of pride and unbelief to resist, reject and suppress the knowledge of God while exploiting His numerous creations and nature under the guise of solving any of man's problems, problems which are mostly caused by sin or hatred for God in the first instance.

Where purpose is not known, abuse is inevitable. Corruption *cannot* solve the problem of corruption, for *in man dwells no good thing.* To avoid this form of degeneration and the pride which results from being puffed up through secular knowledge, we are told, that only a just or a God-fearing man can truly handle knowledge in a balanced way without derailing to the right or the left or mixing things up.

> Give instruction to a wise man, and he will
> be yet wiser: teach a just man, and he will
> increase in learning. The fear of the LORD
> is the beginning of wisdom: and the
> knowledge of the holy is understanding.
> (Proverbs 9:9-10)

By implication, only just men are aware that …*the fear of the LORD is the beginning of wisdom: and the knowledge of the holy is understanding.* And that this kind of knowledge is the true light and the foundation for true love.

## The Knowledge of Good and Evil

> But of the tree of the knowledge of good
> and evil, thou shalt not eat of it: for in the
> day that thou eatest thereof thou shalt surely
> die. (Genesis 2:17)

In summary, man's ability to love properly died the moment he ate this fruit of the knowledge of good and evil, his innocence was taken and his reasoning and emotions were corrupted. A true understanding of the world and how to use the world or solve the problems of the world must begin from and be solidly built upon as well as anchor on the knowledge of God, otherwise, degeneration, exploitation and more and more wickedness and godlessness is what will ultimately result. I have said this before, I'll repeat it again, a knowledgeable man who does not know or fear God will easily use his knowledge as a weapon against fellow humans, he will manipulate everything to his favour and enslave his very own kind, nation, household, colleagues and indeed everyone he is capable of using to further his selfish whims.

Conclusively, it is clear that man cannot escape or be free from darkness except if he encounters God's great light. This is the only heaven-sanctioned way men of all ages are set free from the powers of darkness. In God's light, our dark sides are exposed and cured and we become part and parcel of God's great light, this is how mortal man is able to beam or radiate love. If all I have said to this point is still a bit unclear because (as some would argue), *"these ideas of/about God are all abstract"*, then, rejoice, because God has not only revealed His love to us through His intrinsic attributes, He has also tangibly and bodily revealed His love to us in the person of Jesus Christ, His only begotten Son. To know love in the flesh, God took on flesh in the person of Christ. He came down to practically show us what love is like. Christ *is God's physical representation, the express image of His person.* Anyone who looks to Christ will without fail see God.

> Who being the brightness of his glory, and the express image of his person, and upholding all things by the word of his power, when he had by himself purged our sins, sat down on the right hand of the Majesty on high; (Hebrews 1:3)

In part two of our study, we shall be looking at the Ministry of Jesus Christ, God (Love) incarnate.

*Chapter Seven*

## Chapter Precepts

1.  True Light begins with Divine Encounter
2.  There is a need for all to pursue knowledge in all its forms, because humanity cannot reach its potentials in a state of ignorance.
3.  Scientific knowledge or the knowledge of how things work must however be hinged upon the knowledge and reverential fear of God because,
4.  The knowledge of good and evil, separate from the Holy one of Israel will only lead to more and more ungodliness
5.  Wherever men attempt to separate the knowledge and fear of the Holy One of Israel from His creations, through science experiments or social experiments or any experiment at all, love disappears and evil and wickedness will become the order of the say
6.  The pursuit of God and the knowledge of His word is the secret to accumulating the power of love.

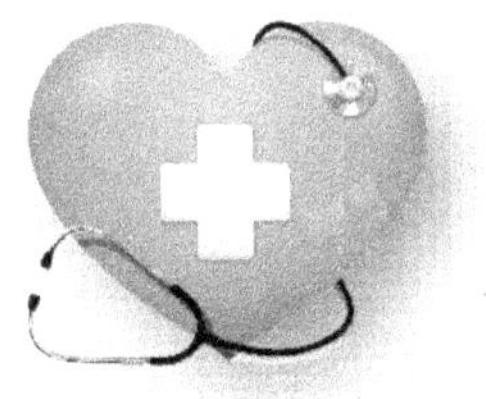

PART TWO

*The Person and Ministry
of Jesus Christ*

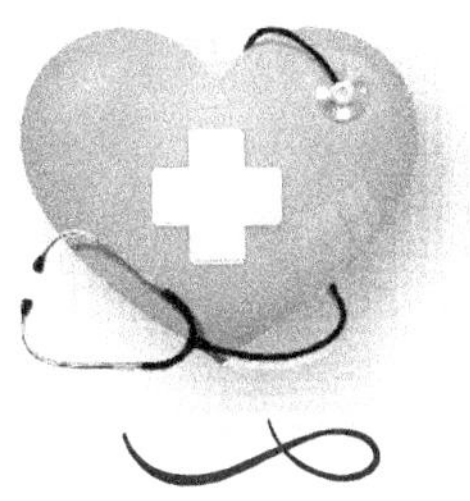



# *Christ: Love Manifested!*

For in him dwelleth all the fulness of the Godhead bodily. (Colossians 2:9)

As earlier noted, God is the one to seek if love is the objective. The problem however lies in the fact that for the natural man, it is not natural to seek after God. Man is more favourably disposed to carnal or worldly pursuits and sees no need for the pursuit of God. His proclivity and preoccupation is to *love the world, and the things that are in the world* (1 John 2:15). He'll rather be religious than godly.

At the peak of worldliness and depravity, satanic ideas and ideologies easily come to the fore in men. It is not uncommon at this time to find that some hold the damning view that there is no God because (as they say), God is not tangible or there is no empirical evidence that He exists because He has not been seen with the physical eyes and cannot be seen with the same. Some erroneously think that atheism as a philosophical movement started with Friedrich Nietzsche, the bible proves otherwise. Atheism is almost as old as man; it is therefore not a result or product of modernism as some would have us believe. As far back as the Old Testament, atheism had gained ground among depraved men. It was so prominent in King David's time that twice in the book of Psalms, King David referred to this kind of thinking as utter foolishness.

> The fool hath said in his heart, **There is no God.** They are corrupt, they have done abominable works, there is none that doeth good. (Psalms 14:1; 53:1)

He also shows us a mystery; he draws our attention to a common denominator among most atheists - Moral Bankruptcy! He says to us that all who profess that there is no God are mostly corrupt, and lacking love. As a result, they do abominable or detestable or repugnant works and the reason for this is simply because they have not known God.

As I mentioned earlier, good deeds or acts of true love are a function of being born of God and knowing God. It derives from encountering God's great light and becoming one with it through faith. Anyone who has no faith in a holy Gd who epitomises love will be full of have and evil deed because he would have excused himself from accountability. This is why faith in God is one of the most important ingredients of love, The fear of the Lord is the foundation for true love.

> But without faith it is impossible to please him: for he that cometh to God must believe that he is, and that he is a rewarder of them that diligently seek him. (Hebrews 11:6)

If we know God, we will place our faith in Him and as a result, we will become people who not only do acts of love but also people who dwells in love. Anyone with the idea that God does not exist has been robbed of his/her capacity to be reconciled to God. Atheism in scripture equals to foolishness because God is active in the lives of all who put their faith in Him. Atheism is nothing but a classic example of foolishness. It is the reason for many troubles.

> For the eyes of the LORD run to and fro throughout the whole earth, to shew himself strong in the behalf of them whose heart is perfect toward him. Herein thou hast done foolishly: therefore from henceforth thou shalt have wars. (2 Chronicles 16:9)

Aside from atheism, another group of "thinkers" are of the view that although God exists, He is withdrawn.

They believe He is far away and cannot be seen or related with. Happily, they are also wrong on all counts! God who is Love, is not hidden or withdrawn, as being withdrawn or hidden is not in His character. Remember, He is Light and in Him is no darkness at all, according to 1 John 1:5.

Also, remember that even when the natural man makes all the efforts to seek God in the flesh through his own religiosity, he always fails because ...*the natural man receiveth not the things of the Spirit of God: for they are foolishness unto him: neither can he know them, because they are spiritually discerned.* (1 Corinthians 2:14). This inadequacy is what gives rise to superstitions, false religions, syncretism, the worship of false gods, animism, and the worship of the elements such as water, the stars, the moon, the sun, thunder, fire, earth, air, trees, carved images, mountains, and natural phenomenon.

The natural man gets lost seeking God. He is lost in sin and trespasses and is eternally lost without a divine search and rescue initiative. The only solution to man's dilemma is for God to seek him.

Happily, we are here told that this is exactly what God did. Remember, earlier in chapter three, we saw that God owns the motive, the means and the method of love.

> Beloved, let us love one another: for love is of God; and every one that loveth is born of God, and knoweth God. He that loveth not

knoweth not God; for God is love. And we have known and believed the love that God hath to us. God is love; and he that dwelleth in love dwelleth in God, and God in him. (1 John 4:7-8,16

These motive, means and method were listed as follows:
a. **The Motive** - *love is of God* – Meaning, Love belongs to God, i.e., He is the brain behind love
b. **The Means** – *every one that loveth is born of God* – i.e., only God's children have the power to love the right way. This means that until a person is born of God, true love is impossible for him, even when he puts his best foot forward every single time.
c. **The Method** - *and knoweth* – i.e., the knowledge of God, His character, intrinsic attributes and provisions and requirements.

All three must converge and unite to make love possible, they are inseparable and are only fulfilled in God. God is however a Spirit and does not live in the flesh like mortals, however, because of His loving nature, He did the unthinkable, He came down to man in the person of Christ.

Therefore if any man be in Christ, he is a new creature: old things are passed away; behold, all things are become new. And all things are of God, who hath <u>reconciled us to himself by Jesus Christ,</u> and hath given to

> us the ministry of reconciliation; To wit, that
> <u>God was in Christ</u>, reconciling the world
> unto himself, not imputing their trespasses
> unto them; and hath committed unto us the
> word of reconciliation. (2 Corinthians 5:17-
> 19)

Anyone searching for God can now easily find Him in the person of Christ for in him is fulfilled these three essential requirements of love. God practically revealed His motive, means and method of love in the person of Christ. By implication, Christ is our perfect embodiment of God's love in human flesh.

> In this was manifested the love of God
> toward us, because that <u>God sent his only
> begotten Son into the world,</u> that we might
> live through him. <u>Herein is love</u>, not that we
> loved God, but that he loved us, and sent
> his Son to be the propitiation for our sins. I
> John 4:9-10

God has manifested or directed His love toward us by sending Christ Jesus as the reconnector *through whom* we might live and without whom mankind is doomed. He came into the world but unfortunately, the world knew Him not, but all who recognise Him in Christ are given the *power* to BECOME the SONS of God

> He was in the world, and the world was
> made by him, and the world knew him not.

> He came unto his own, and his own received him not. But as many as received him, to them gave he power to become the sons of God, even to them that believe on his name: (John 1:10-12)

So, God has done the needful in order for us be reconnected to Him. Even when we fail to seek Him or see a need for a relationship with Him, He reached out to us and came down to us. He came near, even to the extent of waiting on us. He is at the door, knocking.

> Behold, I stand at the door, and knock: if any man hear my voice, and open the door, I will come in to him, and will sup with him, and he with me. (Revelation 3:20)

We now have free and unhindered access to light in the person of Christ. Halleluiah!

> Again, a new commandment I write unto you, which thing is true in him and in you: because the darkness is past, and the true light now shineth. (1 John 2:8)

Yes! Darkness is past and the true light now shines. God's love is now manifest and all can be reconnected. God is aware of man's inability to do this unaided; this explains why He never calls us to self-censorship, nor to personal efforts of piety. Rather, He calls us into a union, a relationship, if we please. He does not only call; He translates the called. He brings us to a new and living way in Christ so that we might live through Him. This is not about us and what we can do; rather, it is all about Him and what He has predetermined to do for us and in us. His intent is that we might live through Him and not through our own efforts, wisdom or intellect.

> Having predestinated us unto the adoption of children by Jesus Christ to himself, <u>according to the good pleasure of his will</u>, (Ephesians 1:5)

> In whom also we have obtained an inheritance, being predestinated <u>according to the purpose of him who worketh all things after the counsel of his own will</u>: (Ephesians 1:11)

Why is it so important for us to live through Him and not through anything else? The reason is simple: God (love) is incarnate in Christ. It is in Christ that God's motive, means and method converge into one tangible historic figure. God's Love literally walked this earth in the person of Christ. He is the way to God. Thus, whatever we do without Him can never and will never meet God's standards or result to love. Christ affirmed this truth when He told His disciples point blank:

> I am the vine, ye are the branches: He that abideth in me, and I in him, the same bringeth forth much fruit: for without me ye

can do nothing. (John 15:5)

In other words, *if you must bear fruit, (especially the fruit of love), stay connected to me.* Since Christ is the original Creator (John 1:3), He is the Vine; therefore, He alone has the capacity to supply the needs of the branches. He knows how best to supply the needed nutrients to every branch so that it can be healthy enough to bear fruit. He knows our weaknesses. He is aware of the fact that no matter how healthy looking a branch is, the moment it detaches itself from the Vine, it is automatically cut off from necessary supplies. He knows that no matter how passionate and willing it is to bear fruit, it cannot; instead, it dries up. This further explains why by strength no man shall prevail.

Don't get tired of hearing this truth: without a strong connection to the author of love, man's love endeavours cannot and will not augur well in the end. To remedy the situation, God sent His only begotten Son (the original creator of all things) into the world that we might live through him.

Dearly beloved, 1 John 4:9-10 is God's solution to all of man's problems. It is not complicated or confusing, and it does not require too much exegesis. God is love, everyone who wants to practice true love MUST be born of God and MUST know God. All these are only reachable in Christ. It is simple and to the point – the one and only way the fruit of love will ever show up in a man's life is to *live through Him.* The only way wickedness, disappointments, heartbreaks and deceptions will disappear among men is for men to *live through Him*. The only way politicians and all those in authority will be truly productive and serve others selflessly, bringing wealth and well-being to their citizens is for them to *live through Him*. The only way men and women can build lasting love relationships is *to live through Him*. The only way to avoid fleshly lusts, adultery, fornication, rape, lasciviousness and all other moral bankruptcy is to *live through Him*. The way of joy, peace, safety, progress, development, abundance and justice is to *live through Him*. Nothing else will work other than the Creator's solution; no idea, invention, ideology, political or economic theory works better. Only one thing is required of us all, and only one thing is needful – we must choose to "live through Him!" Anyone who is not conformed to the image of Christ will be conformed to the image of the Devil and will remain under the power of darkness.

> For whom he did foreknow, he also did predestinate **to be conformed to the image of his Son,** that he might be the firstborn among many brethren. Moreover whom he did predestinate, them he also called: and whom he called, them he also justified: and whom he justified, them he also glorified. (Romans 8:29-30)

If it is love we seek to attain, it is Christ we must look to. Becoming like Christ must therefore be our utmost priority because Christ is the only way to God! He is the fulfilment of God's motive, means and method.

> (Colossians 2:9)  For in him dwelleth all the fulness of the Godhead bodily.

> And to know the love of Christ, which passeth knowledge, that ye might be filled with all the fulness of God. (Ephesians 3:19)

To know Christ is to be filled with all the fulness of God – Jesus Christ is the way of love!

Every journey has its routes and if you are meant to be heading for the United States but board a flight heading for Amsterdam in Holland, you may never get to your destination until you do the right thing. Although there may be many routes to our earthly destinations, when it comes to God (love), Jesus Christ alone is the way.

## Chapter Precepts

1. At the peak of worldliness and depravity, satanic ideas and ideologies easily come to the fore in men.
2. These ideas and worldviews are signs that the natural man cannot seek God
3. Ideologies such as atheism and that of a withdrawn God is untrue because,
4. God has literally or empirically manifested Himself and directed His love towards us by sending Christ Jesus as the re-connector *through whom* we might live and without whom mankind is doomed.
5. Every journey has its routes Christ is the only way to God!

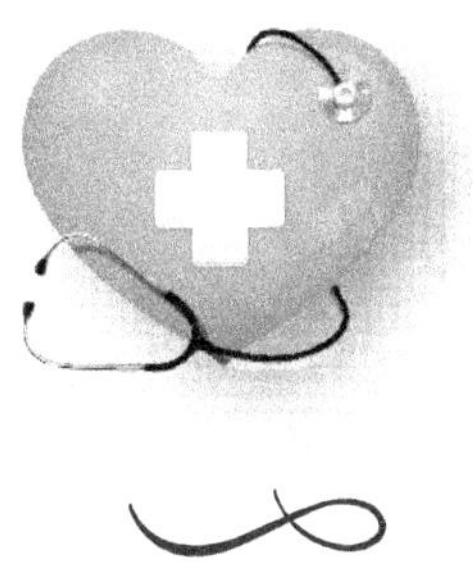

# CHAPTER NINE
## *Christ: The Only Way*

The logical question to ask is why is Christ the only way? Many will argue that it is fatalistic to claim that only Christ has the solution to man's numerous problems or the way to God, especially since there are many religions in the world with many grandiose teachings and many inspiring men and women of wisdom. What about the many great scientists, thinkers, politicians and philosophers of this world? What about the many wonderful ideologies and worldviews that could also be tried? Why then do Christians insist that Christ alone is the Way? Here are your answers:

## 1.  The Need for A Saviour

The first irrefutable reason why Christ is the way is the fact that there is only one way leading to the Father, and we have all missed it, according to Romans 3:12: "They are all gone out of the way" and Romans 3:23 "For all have sinned, and come short of the glory of God."

How did this happen? It started or began in Adam as succinctly captured in 1Corinthians15:2a.

## For as in Adam all die…

After the fall of man in Genesis, he died spiritually and missed the way. Consequently, in Adam, man's nature was corrupted and he became a career sinner. He started to invent and follow his own ways instead of the way of the Master. In his search for restoration, he invented many ways. In no time, he went totally rogue, taking to drugs, sinful pleasures, barbaric religions, satanic philosophies, damnable ideologies, etc., to no avail. The things he thought would make him better made him even worse.

> And God saw that the wickedness of man was great in the earth, and that every imagination of the thoughts of his heart was only evil continually. (Genesis 6:5)

It got so bad that it grieved God's heart.

> And it repented the Lord that he had made

man on the earth, and it grieved him at his heart. (Genesis 6:7)

In no time, the hope of ever finding the way back to God by himself was totally lost because none was spared or left who wasn't corrupt. Romans 3:10-12 says

> As it is written, There is none righteous, no, not one: There is none that understandeth, there is none that seeketh after God. They are all gone out of the way, they are together become unprofitable; there is none that doeth good, no, not one.

Apostle Paul, using his past sinful condition (i.e., his experience before salvation) to describe all who are yet to be redeemed by Christ says in Romans 7:18-20

> "For I know that in me (that is, in my flesh,) dwelleth no good thing: for to will is present with me; but how to
>
> perform that which is good I find not. For the good that I would I do not: but the evil which I would not, that I do. Now if I do that I would not, it is no more I that do it, but sin that dwelleth in me."

Every man has a conscience. We all have the knowledge of good and evil. However, the power to choose good over evil is no longer there. So, it is crystal clear from these portions of Scripture that man is trapped in sins and trespasses, and without a Saviour, even when the will to do right, act right or love is present, the power to do so is inevitably missing.

None is exempt; all men are in a state of death without Christ's salvation. A corpse cannot take or give love; he is totally helpless and degenerating. If he is not redeemed (resurrected), you are only wasting your precious time on decomposing flesh. All men born after Adam's order are dead. This means that they need the Saviour who has power over death and can reverse the damage done by the sting of death. They need more than mere religion, a charismatic prophet or a leader. Man needs more than make-up or cosmetics. He needs the Resurrection and the Life, and only Christ bears that title in heaven, on earth and underneath the earth:

> Jesus said unto her, I am the resurrection, and the life: he that believeth in me, though he were dead, yet shall he live (John 11:25),

The title, The Resurrection and The Life is not just another bogus claim. Jesus is the only being who both raised the dead and foretold His death and resurrection and pulled it off. See John 10:15-18.

By that unique act, He became the firstborn from the dead (i.e., the first person to resurrect and never to die again; the only one who has power over death and power to raise the dead) - Colossians 1:18.

Only Christ has the keys of hell and death, (Revelations 1:18). Consequently, and happily too, 1Corinthians 15:22b tells us gleefully

…in Christ shall all be made alive.

This explains why being born again is a necessity. Everyone born to natural parents must be born a second time through the resurrected Christ. Until a person is born of Christ, he remains spiritually dead. You must have heard about being born again:

> Jesus answered and said unto him, Verily, verily, I say unto thee, Except a man be born again, he cannot see the kingdom of God – John 3:3

Pay close attention to these words of Christ: **"Verily, verily** and **Except** *Verily* means certainly, emphatically, surely, unquestionably, assuredly, without doubt, or undoubtedly. This makes being born again the only route to God's Kingdom. It means that nothing else can lead a man to God's kingdom where he is able to access the power of love or the power to love except being born again. The only key that unlocks the door to heaven is salvation through Christ. Remember, another word for being born again is being redeemed from the state of corruption occasioned by the event of Adam's spiritual death who carried the world in his loins - *in Adam, all die.* In him, all are born with a sinful nature. So, no matter how pious a man may be, his piety will still stink to the high heavens. This is because a pious corpse is helpless; it will decompose and stink.

**Except** simply means exclusivity. It means there is no other way round it.

> But we are all as an unclean thing, and all our righteousnesses are as filthy rags; and we all do fade as a leaf; and our iniquities, like the wind, have taken us away. Isaiah 64:6

**but in Christ shall all be made alive.** All means all; everyone; none is exempted. Adam died, so all died. Jesus resurrected, so all who are born through Him are also resurrected.

> Therefore we are buried with him by baptism into death: that like as Christ was raised up from the dead by the glory of the Father, even so we also should walk in newness of life. For if we have been planted together in the likeness of his death, we shall be also in the likeness of his resurrection: Knowing this, that our old man is crucified with him, that the body of sin might be destroyed, that henceforth we should not serve sin - Romans 6:4-6

There you have it! God's provision in Christ covers all of humanity. The whole world's redemption has been provided for in Christ. God's provision of love is for all humanity.

> For God so loved the world, that he gave his only begotten Son, that whosoever believeth in him should not perish, but have everlasting life. For God sent not his Son into the world to condemn the world; but that the world through him might be saved. John 3:16 -17

God is essentially love. He can be trusted. He does not want any to perish.

> The Lord is not slack concerning his promise, as some men count slackness; but is longsuffering to us-ward, not willing that any should perish, but that all should come to repentance. 2Peter 3:9.

God wants ALL to COME to Him, so, He paid the price for ALL. None was left out.

## The Freewill Question

While it is true that the whole world is captured in God's redemptive plan, man was created with free will, and thus has the power of choice. He can choose what to believe and what to disbelieve. God does not and will not force His will on man. However, only "He that believeth on him is not condemned: but he that believeth not is condemned already, because he hath not believed in the name of the only begotten Son of God" - John 3:16 -18.

Consequently, only those who have accepted Christ as their Lord and Saviour and are living through Him will not perish. When the Bible says "he that believeth not is <u>condemned already</u>", this can only mean that he is already dead. Anyway, he died in Adam; so, refusing Christ (The Resurrection and The Life) can only mean choosing Adam (Death). Consequently, it is only natural for a corpse to decompose. To live, however, all must come through Christ and be resurrected. This is the due order; you cannot re-arrange it.

## The Dead Cannot Show Emotions

Anyone who does not put his faith in the atoning work of Christ on Calvary is still dead in sins and trespasses. He has not experienced love, and therefore, cannot give love. Forget about his/her good looks, flashy cars, enviable background, educational achievements, social status or religiosity. S/he is a walking corpse! Like a melting candle, s/he is perishing daily! You do not want to perish with him!

"What if he/she is very religious?" you may ask. Unfortunately, mere religiosity will not suffice. Without fuel in your tank, your willingness to drive your beautiful car is actually an impossible task. If you don't fill the tank, but keep trying to force the engine to run, you will soon run down your battery. So also, without accepting

Christ's salvation, no man can carry on in love. It is practically an exercise in futility; it is a risk not worth taking.

Believe me; no unregenerated man has succeeded in doing so from Genesis to Revelation. The question remained unanswered; and until Jesus appeared on the scene, the puzzle remained unsolved. Even His very disciples had questions. In the book of Matthew chapter 19, from the third verse down to the twelfth, we have an account of how because of lack of salvation or failure to accept Christ's redemption (what the Lord rightly calls hardness of heart), the religious leaders of those days had, according to Finnis Jenins Dakes, *"Permitted divorce on many frivolous grounds, such as careless seasoning of food, causing the husband to eat food which had not been tithed, going into the street with loose or uncombed hair, spinning in the street, loud talk or constant talking on the home, the husband finding one more beautiful than his wife and many other things."*[2]

Jesus however made it clear that the issue with love burnout was none of these things listed above. The real issue why men or women of all ages fail in love is very simple: they are powerless to continue to love the same person in a state of spiritual death or unconsciousness.

Remember, I mentioned earlier that David the Psalmist, a man after God's own heart knew experientially what it means to fail in love. He actually had to learn this lesson

---

[2] Dakes' Annotated Bible, Commentary by Finnis Jennins Dakes

the hard way. Hear him in his own words:

> My flesh and my heart faileth… Psalm 73:26aMen's heart will continue to fail them until they find Christ.

So, the reason why man needs The Saviour is simple - he is lost and cannot find the way without a saviour. He is dead in sins and trespasses; only the Resurrection and Life can restore him.

## 2.　　The Sinlessness of Christ

Although it is true that the Jesus Christ of the Bible is a man, He is not a mere man. He is God incarnate. If He was a mere man, He couldn't have done any better than other great men out there- but this is not the case. Christ in His earthly days was also God incarnate. He was fully God and fully man. This is one of the most important qualifications He possessed as the Saviour of mankind.

He is the Son of God. Like God His father, He is hundred percent God too because everything brings forth according to its kind. Jesus is not God because Christians want Him to be God, without Christians, He will still be God. He was God, He is God, He will always be God.

> Let this mind be in you, which was also in Christ Jesus: Who, being in the form of God, thought it not robbery to be equal

> with God: But made himself of no
> reputation, and took upon him the form of
> a servant, and was made in the likeness of
> men: (Philippians 2:5-7)

According to divine justice, only blood can atone for sin. *And almost all things are by the law purged with blood; and without shedding of blood is no remission.* (Hebrews 9:22)

However, just any blood would not do. A man's sin can only be atoned for by a man's blood. The blood of bulls could only purify the flesh but not the soul -

> For if the blood of bulls and of goats, and
> the ashes of an heifer sprinkling the unclean,
> sanctifieth to the purifying of the flesh:
> Hebrews 9:13

Consequently, man would have been eternally doomed if there was no sinless man whose blood could qualify to atone for His sins and reverse the judgement or sentence of eternal damnation passed upon humanity due to the fall. This is the reason why God became man in the person of Christ and took man's place, paying the penalty of sin – i.e., death in full, and resurrecting for man's justification.

> And I saw a strong angel proclaiming with a
> loud voice, Who is worthy to open the
> book, and to loose the seals thereof?  And
> one of the elders saith unto me, Weep not:

behold, the Lion of the tribe of Juda, the Root of David, hath prevailed to open the book, and to loose the seven seals thereof. Revelations 5:2; 5:5

The one hundred percent man, Christ Jesus in His earthly days was tempted as every other man; yet, He never sinned.

> For we have not an high priest which cannot be touched with the feeling of our infirmities; but was in all points tempted like as we are, yet without sin. (Hebrews 4:15)

Christ Jesus went on to die on the cross of Calvary for our sins and was buried. On the third day, He rose up for our justification. He is our High Priest before God, He is *the Lion of the tribe of Judah, the Root of David,* who *prevailed to open the book and to loose the seven seals thereof.*

This is why I know that the journey to love starts at the foot of Christ's cross.

> Herein is love, not that we loved God, but that he loved us, and sent his Son to be the propitiation for our sins (1 John 4:10)

It is the power or force of God's love that humbled Christ and made Him into a man, just for our redemption. It is this same love that took Christ to the cross. The word of God insists that He is not propitiation but THE very propitiation for the sins of the whole world.

> And he is the propitiation for our sins: and not for ours only, but also for the sins of the whole world. 1 John 2:2)

Dearly beloved, humanity can only overcome Satan and eternal damnation through Christ's shed blood. Nothing else is good enough!

> And they overcame him by the blood of the Lamb, Revelations 12:11a

> And to Jesus the mediator of the new covenant, and to the blood of sprinkling, that speaketh better things than that of Abel. Hebrews 12:24

> Neither by the blood of goats and calves, but by his own blood he entered in once into the holy place, having obtained eternal redemption for us. How much more shall the blood of Christ, who through the eternal Spirit offered himself without spot to God, purge your conscience from dead works to serve the living God? Hebrews 9:12; 14

> In whom we have redemption through his blood, the forgiveness of sins, according to the riches of his grace; Ephesians 1:7

And he was clothed with a vesture dipped in blood: and his name is called The Word of God. Revelations19:13

3.      **Christ's Claims**

The world as we know it has produced many political, philosophical, political or religious leaders. What fascinates men about these leaders of thought most times are their claims, especially the idea that they are God's special envoy to the world, or that they have a unique message to the world, or yet still, that they are the long-awaited messiah. By hook or crook, most of these strange men with their strange claims have gone on to lead many astray. Some even ushered the world into times of great pains, trials and tribulations. Some ended up stirring up wars, hatred, racism, superiority complex, strive, murders, ethnic and tribal clashes, famine, bloodletting, destruction of lives and properties, genocide, infanticide, sexual immoralities, mass hysteria, drug abuse and addiction, suicide and the untimely death, both of themselves and their deceived followers. From the fall till date, there have been countless impostors, who have founded numerous schools of thoughts, religions, theories, ideologies and movements. Some false messiahs existed in the past and even now there are uncountable false prophets, priests and spiritual guides but none of them ever made Christ's claims. Those who claimed to be the way failed woefully when it was time to prove it.

According to Edward N. Gross, *Jesus actually claimed to be*

*God, having divine characteristics like eternity (John 8:58; 17:5), omnipresence (Matt. 18:20; 28:20), and omnipotence (John 5:17; Rev. 1:8). He allowed and commanded worship of himself (John 9:38; Matt. 28:9; John 5:22-23; 14:1). He used and accepted titles belonging only to God (John 1:29, 49;51; 6:35; 20:28). He claimed to be sinless (John 8:46), to speak only truth (John 18:37), and to command the angels of heaven (Matt. 25:31; 26:53). He made promises that only God can keep: to forgive sin (Matt. 9:17), to send the Spirit (John 15:26), to answer prayers (John 14:14), and to give eternal life (John 10:28). His claims to deity were so clear that his opponents sought to kill him for them (John 5:18; 10:33; Matt. 26:63,66).*[3]

In all of human history, only Jesus Christ openly and boldly claimed to be **the way** and successfully backed up His claims with infallible proof. So, another irrefutable proof that Christ is the way lies in His bold and proven claims.

> Jesus saith unto him, I am the way, the truth, and the life: no man cometh unto the Father, but by me. (John 14:6)

That is profound! As noted earlier, some have dared to claim to be a way but none of them ended up backing their claims with infallible proof like Christ did.

Jesus Christ is the way to the Father; He is the one to follow if attaining true love is the goal. Happily, He is

---

[3]Edward N. Gross, Doctrine 101: The Deity of Christ
https://opc.org/new_horizons/NH00/0003d.html

not silent, even today. His voice is the actual voice of wisdom calling out in Proverbs 8. As always, He continues to call out to all wayfarers intending to travel to the destination called Love: "I am the way" – definite article.

Note the difference: Jesus did not claim to be a way; instead, He said He is The Way to the Father - Love. He was not the way; He *is* The Way and He remains the way. His name is THE WAY.

He purposely chose the definite article to describe Himself to the end that none is left in doubt about the fact that that He is not just *a way* but the one and **only Way** to God. His intent is for us to come to the realisation that there is no other way and there can be no other way to God except Him!

Thankfully, His is not a bogus claim, He is not a usurper. Again, we are sure He is the way because He did not stop at merely making the claim. He went on to prove it. How? Through:

a.      **His Death and Resurrection**

History has it that Christ died and resurrected just as he had predicted. He is the first and the only person who foretold his death, defined the reason why He would die and resurrect, and pulled it off. However, nay Sayers and His enemies have always tried to discountenance His death and resurrection to no avail. Christ's death and resurrection is a historical truth. However, for many who continue to ask "how can we be sure that Christ's death is not just a farce or fable cunningly devised by religious bigots?" the overwhelming evidence for Christ's death and resurrection are too numerous to mention. Nonetheless, a concise account is flawlessly captured in this article by Darrel & Cindy deVille on the website, charismanews.com

"... to know Him, and **the power of His resurrection**, and the fellowship of His sufferings, being conformed to His death ..." (Phil. 3:10, MEV).

The apostle Paul expressed that Jesus Christ's resurrection is the cornerstone of our faith in Him (1 Cor. 15:14). And although skeptics have tried to refute this, the evidence for God and the resurrection of Jesus Christ is undeniable, if one is willing to objectively look at all the evidence. The truth is being a believer is not a blind leap of faith but a real relationship with a living God whose fingerprints seem to be everywhere we look.

There are many verifiable facts of the resurrection of Jesus Christ, and the following are only seven of them.

1.   **The empty tomb**. Even the enemies of Christ never denied the empty tomb. And all other explanations, body stolen, He wasn't really dead, and so on, are easily debunked when examined.

2.   **Post-resurrection appearances.** People saw, touched, walked along side, ate with, and listened to Jesus. Hundreds of witnesses (over 500!) saw Him at one time (1 Cor, 15:6), which psychologists confirm could not have been the result of a mass hallucination as some sceptics claim.

The resurrection of Christ was a bodily one. Following His resurrection, He presented Himself as proof that He indeed was alive! He offered Himself to be touched, revealing His crucifixion scars, then eating with the disciples. He presented clear evidence He had risen bodily from the grave.

"... to whom He presented Himself alive after His passion by many infallible proofs, appearing to them for forty days, and speaking concerning the kingdom of God" (Acts 1:3, MEV). This is the only place in the Bible the word "infallible proof" is used. This word means solid proof in a court of law.

3.  **The testimony of women.** The fact that women were the first to discover and testify of the empty tomb and that He had risen is noteworthy because in the Greco-Roman world the testimony of women was not considered reliable. If the gospel writers felt the liberty to make things up, they certainly would not report that women discovered the empty tomb, for that would only weaken their case and cause. They however, reported what they saw with their own eyes, trusting the truth would bear out.

4.  **Transformed lives of disciples.** There is no doubt something very real and dramatic happened that transformed eleven cowardly men, hiding in fear for their lives, into bold outspoken evangelists. These men became willing to risk imprisonment, excommunication, torture, and even death in order to proclaim the resurrection of Jesus Christ in the very city he was crucified! They would not willingly die if they knew this was all a lie. The fact is they knew Christ had indeed risen — they saw Him, talked to Him, touched Him, and ate with Him. Knowing the truth of the resurrection, they were willing to die for Him.

5.  **Birth of the Christian church.** It's evident that something of great significance and supernatural took place that caused the Christian faith to explode in growth in the very city Christ was crucified and buried in. Within a few centuries, from Jerusalem all the way thru the Roman Empire Christianity became the dominant religion, displacing centuries of pagan practices. All this without any modern forms of communication, travel or media. Only something as compelling and persuasive as Jesus' Resurrection could account for such a remarkable transformation.

**6.   James' conversion**. Jesus' half-brother, James was a sceptic until he encountered the risen Christ. As a result, he became a strong leader in the early church.

**7.   Saul's conversion on the road to Damascus.** Some supernatural encounter must have occurred to cause such a radical change in Saul, transforming him from a fanatical hater and persecutor of Christians into the greatest defender, missionary, and evangelist the church has ever known.

## The Truth from Two of the World's Greatest Legal Minds

**a.   Sir Lionel Luckhoo (1914-1997),** considered one of the greatest lawyers in British history. He's recorded in the Guinness Book of World Records as the "World's Most Successful Advocate," with 245 consecutive murder acquittals. He was knighted by Queen Elizabeth II – twice. After his complete examination of the facts, Sir Luckhoo declared: "I humbly add I have spent more than 42 years as a defense trial lawyer appearing in many parts of the world ... I say unequivocally the evidence for the Resurrection of Jesus Christ is so overwhelming that it compels acceptance by proof which leaves absolutely no room for doubt." – Sir Lionel Luckhoo

**b.   Simon Greenleaf (1783-1853)** was one of the founders of Harvard Law School. He authored the authoritative three-volume text, A Treatise on the Law of Evidence (1842), which is still considered "the greatest single authority on evidence in the entire literature of legal procedure." Greenleaf literally wrote the rules of evidence for the U.S. legal system. He was certainly a man who knew how to weigh the facts.

Greenleaf was an atheist until he accepted a challenge by his students to investigate the case for Christ's resurrection.

### Simon Greenleaf Investigation
After personally collecting and examining the evidence based on rules of evidence that he helped establish, Greenleaf

became a Christian and wrote the classic, Testimony of the Evangelists ...after thorough investigation of the resurrection, concluded... "The resurrection of Christ is the most verifiable fact of ancient history" – Simon Greenleaf
What more could be said?"

**SOURCE:**   http://www.charismanews.com/opinion/56077-7-pieces-of-evidence-for-the-resurrection

## 3. The Testimony of Converts

Christianity was birthed after the disciples were baptised with the Holy Ghost on the day of Pentecost as documented in the book of Acts. This was in fulfilment of another of Christ's promise to His disciples before and after His death and resurrection. This event was so profound that the disciples went all out to declare and bear witness to it. Consequently, although Christianity is by faith, this is not an abstract faith. The Christian faith is not placed in an unknown god (Acts 17:23), but in a well-known God. Many have seen and experienced Him and have passed on these testimonies from one generation to the other (See Psalm 44). Death is the ultimate or supreme price many are never willing to pay, no, not even for a matching crime; yet from inception, believers were tortured, beaten and were many times killed because of their testimony about Christ but they refused to be silenced (Acts 4:19). Others though dead, yet keep on speaking loud and clear from their graves (Hebrews 1:4; Hebrews 11). Hear them:

> For we cannot but speak the things which
> we have seen and heard. (Acts 4:20)

> That which was from the beginning, which we have heard, which we have seen with our eyes, which we have looked upon, and our hands have handled, of the Word of life; (For the life was manifested, and we have seen it, and bear witness, and shew unto you that eternal life, which was with the Father, and was manifested unto us;) (That which we have seen and heard declare we unto you, that ye also may have fellowship with us: and truly our fellowship is with the Father, and with his Son Jesus Christ. And we have seen and do testify that the Father sent the Son to be the Saviour of the world.
> (1 John 1:1-3; 4:14)

So, you see, the Christian faith (the claim that Jesus Christ is the way) is not based on the figments of anyone's imagination. It is not based on cunningly devised fables or myths and legends (2Peter 1:16). It is a historical fact that for thousands of years has endured all the rigorous tests it has been subjected to. It remains true all the time, even forevermore. It is scientifically proven and historically accurate. All who experience Christ are liberated - Psalm 12:6

Above all, the most mind-blowing thing about Christ's death on our behalf is the fact that Jesus Christ was not forced to die for our sins. He chose to do so because of His great love for man. Hear Him:

> Greater love hath no man than this, that a man lay down his life for his friends. (John 15:13)"

## Accessing Love

"How then do we access this wonderful provision of God?" you may ask. In simple terms, just like a man in need of a lifesaving surgery, all you need to do is get into God's theatre (operating room) and allow Him transform you from inside out. In the words of Christ, you must be born again.

> Jesus answered and said unto him, Verily, verily, I say unto thee, Except a man be born again, he cannot see the kingdom of God. (John 3:3)

## Love Comes with the Gift of a New Heart

Love is a matter of the heart. Love comes with the gift of a new heart however, made possible by Christ's atoning dead and resurrection. It is solely a by-product of redemption, a package which comes with a spiritual surgical operation where God replaces the old wicked, deceitful and depraved heart with a new heart of love. Love cannot thrive in a stone-cold dead heart because by default, that heart is *deceitful above all things, and desperately wicked: who can know it?* (Jeremiah 17:9). It is depraved and wicked to the extent that even the bearer cannot fully unravel the extent of its wickedness. God is however All Knowing, so He is not unaware of man's predicament. Long before He sent Christ to die for man, the prophet Ezekiel made it abundantly clear; God promised that He would give man a new heart, and replace his stony, deceitful and desperately wicked heart with a living one.

> And I will give them one heart, and I will put a new spirit within you; and I will take the stony heart out of their flesh, and will give them an heart of flesh: Ezekiel 11:19)

See also Ezekiel 18:31, Ezekiel 36:26.
 We all agree that love is a matter of the heart. Consequently, a heartless soul cannot give it. When we say a man is born again, what we mean is that he now has a brand-new heart. Halleluiah! All who realise their need for a new heart can now access it freely through Christ. One more time, salvation or accepting Christ as your Lord and Saviour is the gate pass to a new heart.

If you want to experience true love and receive the power of love, this is a good time to embrace Christ Jesus, the only Saviour of humanity; harden not your heart. Today is the day of salvation and the accepted time. Go on your knees and say the following prayers with all sincerity:

*Lord Jesus, I realise I am a sinner deserving death and that in fact, I died in Adam. Nevertheless, I believe by your precious blood you have paid the price for my sins. Upon my acceptance of your finished work at Calvary, I humbly confess my sins today and ask for your forgiveness. Give me a new life and a new beginning. Your Word says that those who come to you, you will in no wise cast out. I come to you today. Write my name in the Book of Life and forgive all my failings. I believe I am forgiven and saved. I accept your love and thank you for forgiving me. In Jesus' precious name I pray. Amen.*

If you said that prayer sincerely, welcome back to life from the land of the dead and decomposing. You are now the redeemed of the Lord. You are ransomed, blood washed and loved. You are safe and saved from condemnation. You have taken the first step in the right direction. You now have a new heart; the heart of flesh. However, there is more; because we all know that anyone who has just been to the operation theatre for a major surgery would need time to recuperate fully. Also, there are specific (prescribed) meditations (including vitamins and supplements) needed on the journey to full recovery. The journey to love has just begun. There are other important encounters to have on this journey because God is triune, and He manifests Himself in three distinct persons, through Christ:

> For there are three that bear record in heaven, the Father, the Word, and the Holy Ghost: and these three are one. And there are three that bear witness in earth, the Spirit, and the water, and the blood: and these three agree in one. (1John 5:7-8)

The Godhead is made of the Father God Almighty, The Word is Christ and the Holy Ghost is His Spirit. All three are equal, according the scriptures.

## Chapter Precepts

1. Christ is the only way because,
   - Humanity is lost and needs a Saviour
   - The Saviour must be sinless because a guilty party in a crime is not qualified to bail his fellow criminal
   - Only Christ is sinless
   - Christ was not forced to die for humanity, he voluntarily and willingly did so.
   - 

2. He did not only die for our sins, He also resurrected for our justification

3. His resurrection claim is not fictional, it is historical with evidence. His disciples saw His resurrected body. The tomb is empty and Christ is alive today. They were witnesses of His ascension to heaven and were willing to die for their claims

4. Love Comes with the gift of a new heart however, made possible by Christ's atoning dead and resurrection. Consequently, a heartless soul cannot give it.

5. Man is a free moral agent; he has the freewill to

accept God's offer of salvation in Christ or to reject it. So, while it is true that the sins of the whole world have been atoned for, only those who accepts Christ's offer will be saved, the rest are doomed for rejecting God's provision for their salvation.

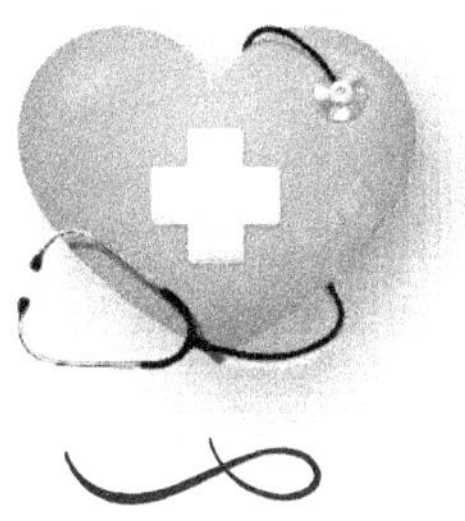

# CHAPTER TEN
## *Christ the Word of God*

God, who at sundry times and in divers manners spake in time past unto the fathers by the prophets, Hath in these last days spoken unto us by his Son, whom he hath appointed heir of all things, by whom also he made the worlds; Who being the brightness of his glory, and the express image of his person, and upholding all things by the word of his power, when he had by himself purged our sins, sat down on the right hand of the Majesty on high; being made so much better than the angels, as he hath by inheritance obtained a more excellent name than they. (Hebrews 1:1-4)

The ministry of Christ is yet incomplete if we neglect or leave out His role as the Word of God. In the Old Testament, God revealed Himself to the world through miracles, signs and wonders. He was seen speaking through the prophets and His ministers. The God of love is not a silent God but an expressive God. If He made us with the capacity to speak and express ourselves in more ways than one, He can speak and express Himself whichever way or form He chooses. Throughout man's existence and history, He spoke and continues to speak today. However, unlike the ways He spoke in the Old Testament, today, He speaks primarily through Christ. Jesus Christ is God's final word to mankind. After Him is judgement. Anyone who encounters Christ encounters God's Word in the flesh. We are told in Scripture that although Christ is the only begotten Son, He is also the Word.

> For there are three that bear record in heaven, the Father, the Word, and the Holy Ghost: and these three are one. 1 John 5:7

Jesus Christ is here referred to as the Word of God because:

a. He is the one through whom God (Elohim) spoke the universe into existence. The word *"Logos"* is the Greek word for *word, reason, speech* or *principle.* John in his book used it to describe the person and ministry of Christ. *Logos,* in John 1:1-14 embodies the idea of a "divine reason" or "the mind of God." By implication, John was communicating to his mostly Greek speaking audience whose understanding of *logos* up until then was more of philosophical than tangible that beyond the abstract, the cosmic Christ has entered into our earthly realm for the purpose of bringing the divine life and lifestyle into the earthly realm. He is not abstract neither is He a mere philosophical thought.

- **Jesus is eternal** because He was with God prior to His earthly advent – *In the beginning was the Word, and the Word was with God, and the Word was God. The same was in the beginning with God.* John 1:1-2
- **Jesus is God the Creator -** *All things were made by him; and without him was not any thing made that was made.* (John 1:3)
- **Jesus is the Giver of Life** - *In him was life; and the life was the light of men.* (John 1:4)
- **Jesus (God's Logos) became Flesh and dwelt among us** -) *And the Word was made flesh, and dwelt among us, (and we beheld his glory, the glory as of the only begotten of the Father,) full of grace and truth.* (John 1:14

Basically, what this scripture is affirming to us is that God has revealed Himself physically to mankind through Christ. If we want to know grace and truth, we must look to Christ; if we want the life of God or the love of God, it is fully expressed in Christ.

Who being the brightness of his glory, and

> the express image of his person, and upholding all things by the word of his power, when he had by himself purged our sins, sat down on the right hand of the Majesty on high; (Hebrews 1:3)

In Hebrews 1:3 above, His mission on earth is succinctly captured – to fix His original creation that was once damaged through sin; to purge our sins and teach us His way of life - upholding all things by the word of his power. This means that without His word, nothing is sustainable, and nothing can last. This is because the creation was made possible by the instrumentality of His powerful words. Empty human words cannot fix man's problems on earth. God's powerful Word is the solution. Christ is the full expression of God's word and power. Consequently, anyone who needs to hear from God today or see God's power can actually do so in the person of Christ - God-incarnate.

Christ is God's final word to mankind, and beyond the metaphysical, Christ walked this earth in the flesh. He did this primarily to identify with us and show us how God literally intends for us to live our earthly lives. We may not see God with our physical eyes nor ear Him the way we hear our family and friends because He is a Spirit, yet we can see and hear Him literally the way we see and hear our physical relatives through His physical manifestation in the person of Christ - *Looking unto Jesus the author and finisher of our faith; who for the joy that was set before him endured the cross, despising the shame, and is set down at the right hand of the throne of God.* (Hebrews 12:2)

No one else may understand or empathise with us in times of crises; yet, Christ knows exactly how we feel and understands our pains because He Himself was once in the flesh like we are, in crisis or temptation, we can study His life as documented in the bible for direction and inspiration.

> Forasmuch then as the children are partakers of flesh and blood, he also himself likewise took part of the same; that through death he might destroy him that had the power of death, that is, the devil; And deliver them who through fear of death were all their lifetime subject to bondage. For verily he took not on him the nature of angels; but he took on him the seed of Abraham. Wherefore in all things it behoved him to be made like unto his brethren, that he might be a merciful and faithful high priest in things pertaining to God, to make reconciliation for the sins of the people. For in that he himself hath suffered being tempted, he is able to succour them that are tempted. (Hebrews 2:14-18)

Christ is God's perfect model for humanity. Christ is God's standard to look to, not self or fallible men. Christ is the one to emulate in love.

> For we have not an high priest which
> cannot be touched with the feeling of our
> infirmities; but was in all points tempted
> like as we are, yet without sin. (Hebrews
> 4:15)

All of our questions are answered in Him. The best mentor a person can have is Christ. Man's best motivator should be none other than Christ. Christ is God's manual for our everyday living. He is God's word that we must study to be like. Since He is God's word in the flesh, His lifestyle on earth is the full expression of the Power of Love. Every man who studies the life of Christ and applies His principles naturally radiates love. God is love, and Christ is His word made flesh and His full expression. Embracing Christ's lifestyle is thus embracing a lifestyle of love.

Again, Christ is God's word because the entire Scriptures (God's inspired written word), testify of or point to Him. *Search the scriptures; for in them ye think ye have eternal life: and they are they which testify of me.* (John 5:39). This is why we must be friends with our Bible. To study and live according to the dictates of the Bible is to study and live as Christ lived. No one can go wrong in love studying and obeying scriptures.

The shortest cut to love is to embrace the truths of the Bible.

1. **The Bible represents light,** - *Thy word is a lamp*

2. *unto my feet, and a light unto my path.* (Psalms 119:105)

Remember, Jesus Christ is the Light of the World – *Then spake Jesus again unto them, saying, I am the light of the world: he that followeth me shall not walk in darkness, but shall have the light of life.* (John 8:12)

3. **It points us to the Way** - *I will instruct thee and teach thee in the way which thou shalt go: I will guide thee with mine eye.* (Psalms 32:8)

Again, He (Jesus), is also the Way - *Jesus saith unto him, I am the way, the truth, and the life: no man cometh unto the Father, but by me.* (John 14:6)

What this means is that the whole Scriptures form a document about Christ. This is why Christ and the Bible are both called the word of God. Christ actually insists that His words are *spirit* and *life.*

> It is the spirit that quickeneth; the flesh profiteth nothing: the words that I speak unto you, they are spirit, and they are life. (John 6:63)

Studying and living by Christ's word therefore equals to living in the Spirit of Christ. Herein is love manifested. The kind of life that is obtainable here is not the normal, carnal life but the very life of God, a life of love. In essence, the closer we get to the Bible, the closer we would be to God; and because Christ is the theme of the Bible, we would not walk in darkness nor depart from the way. This is the way to sustain love.

This is why the apostle instructed us to,

> Let the word of Christ dwell in you richly in all wisdom; teaching and admonishing one another in psalms and hymns and spiritual songs, singing with grace in your hearts to the Lord. (Colossians 3:16)

When the word of Christ dominates our hearts, the character of Christ naturally becomes our lifestyle because Christ Himself is God's word manifested in human flesh. Christ is the standard of God's love and His example is our high calling. His lifestyle is what we are called to emulate, and His words are our earthly constitution, which we are saved to live by. Without the word of God, the life of Christ is impossible.

In Chapters 11 and 12, we shall examine more explicitly the place of the written word of God in our love life. In the meantime, we must study another ministry of Christ which is the fact that He is the Baptiser with The Holy Spirit.

> For there are three that bear record in heaven, the Father, the Word, and the Holy Ghost: and these three are one. 1 John 5:7

## Chapter Precepts

1. Christ is God's final statement to humanity. After Christ, humanity will be judged. In the past, God spoke to mankind through priests, prophets and other agents but today, His final word is Jesus Christ.

2. Christ knows exactly how we feel and understands our pains because He Himself was once in the flesh like we are, in crisis or temptation, we can study His life as documented in the bible for direction and inspiration.

3. Again, Christ is God's word. the entire Scriptures (God's inspired written word), testify of or point to Him. *Search the scriptures; for in them ye think ye have eternal life: and they are they which testify of me.* (John 5:39).

4. When the word of Christ dominates our hearts, the character of Christ naturally becomes our lifestyle because Christ Himself is God's word manifested in human flesh. Christ is the standard of God's love and His example is our high calling. His lifestyle is what we are called to emulate, and His words are our

earthly constitution, which we are saved to live by.

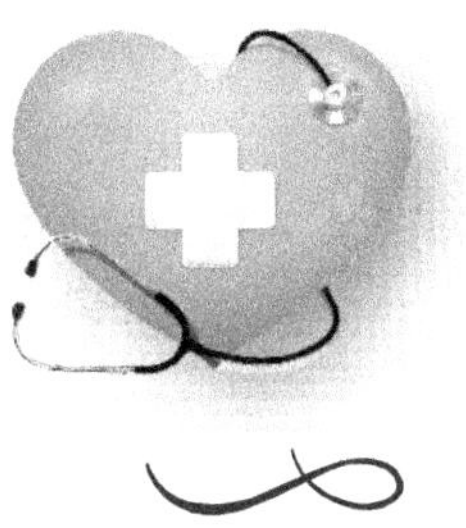



# *The Holy Spirit:*
# *Treasure in Earthen Vessels*

Lest we forget, this book is about the Power of Love. So far, we have seen that God is the owner of all powers, and that He is also love. Also, we have seen that He manifested this love to us in Christ, and that Christ is the only way because He alone is the sinless lamb whose blood qualifies to propitiate and atone for our sins. He alone is able to save us from our sins and its consequences. He is also the way because He is the one who keeps us saved. He is the very Word of

God by whom God made all things and without whom nothing was made. Christ is God speaking to man now. Moreover, Christ's ministry also includes the fact that He is the baptizer with the Holy Ghost.

> I indeed baptize you with water unto repentance: but he that cometh after me is mightier than I, whose shoes I am not worthy to bear: he shall baptize you with the Holy Ghost, and with fire. Matthew 3:11

Without Christ, the Holy Ghost wouldn't have come and without the Holy Ghost, no man can bear the fruit of love. Although Christ's disciples were born again and probably water-baptised, that alone did not grant them the needed power to become all that God wanted them to become. Until they were baptised with the Holy Ghost, they remained somewhat weak and powerless. The Lord knew how important being Spirit baptised is if anyone is to manifest God's power; so, He instructed His disciples to wait in Jerusalem until they were able to receive power. He COMMANDED them to do or say nothing, until they were duly filled (fuelled) or baptised with the Holy Spirit.

> But ye shall <u>receive power</u>, after that the Holy Ghost is come upon you: and ye shall be witnesses unto me both in Jerusalem, and in all Judaea, and in Samaria, and unto the uttermost part of the earth. Acts 1:8

This means that the Holy Spirit is the actual Power of God. Power is received, *after,* not *before* the Holy Ghost is come upon a person. When we accept Christ, and get Spirit-baptised, what naturally happens is that like collector panels we accumulate power; a very uncommon kind of power that the world cannot know or understand. This is the Power of Love or the Power to Love.

## The Fruit of The Spirit is Love

By now, you should have realised that love goes beyond mere feelings; it is a type of fruit, which can only be found on the tree called "The Holy Spirit." When the bible says *the fruit of the Spirit is love,* in the book of Galatians 5:22, what it means is that what is obtainable when a man is filled with the Holy Spirit is *love.* As long as we are in the flesh, the temptation to follow fleshly lusts will remain but when we *Walk in the Spirit,* we *shall not fulfil the lust of the flesh,* Galatians 5:16. Every tree produces after its kind; so also, is love. While they may look alike, expecting plantain from a banana tree will end in disappointment because that is a misplaced expectation. Similarly, expecting love from a soul devoid of the Holy Spirit can only end in frustration. Love is not obtainable elsewhere; it is derived from the Holy Spirit - Galatians 5:22-24.

This means that until we are engrafted into the tree of love, bearing the fruit of love remains a mere wish; it is impossible!

The gospel of Jesus Christ is the good news of salvation. It is called *the good news* because as earlier noted, there was a bad incident in the garden that led to the fall of man and his unfortunate separation from God (see Genesis 3). Consequently, he disqualified and disconnected himself and was duly rejected in the beloved, i.e., he became orphaned or disconnected from his own source and was driven out. This had to be so because of God's justice – God hates sin. He hated it then, and still hates it now and evermore. His eyes are too holy; He cannot live with it. In Habakkuk 1:13a, Habakkuk said concerning God – "*Thou art* of purer eyes than to behold evil, and canst not look on iniquity…"

Undoubtedly, this was indeed *bad news*! It caused a contradiction of some sort. God loves man, yet he hates sin; man is sinful and has become a slave to it. Sin became an addiction or obsession of sort; it became man's new nature. Yet, God is holy and cannot live with or condone sin. He had to look away! From then on, sin multiplied among men and everyone born was born preloaded with an incredible proclivity and capacity for sin.

> Behold, I was shapen in iniquity; and in sin did my mother conceive me. (Psalms 51:5),

It became so bad, man could only walk *in the vanity of their mind, Having the understanding darkened, being alienated from the life of God through the ignorance that is in them, because of the blindness of their heart:* (Ephesians 4:17-18)

Although God dislikes sin, He loves man. Consequently, there was a need to separate the world (man) He loves, from the sinful nature (spirit of sin). As earlier noted, God alone could solve this problem. He didn't have to do it, but happily, His loving nature made Him do it. He wasted no time in setting a comprehensive plan of salvation in motion. This is true because we are told that Christ was actually prepared ready in the Spirit realm where God dwells before the foundation of the world but was manifested at the appointed time.

> Forasmuch as ye know that ye were not redeemed with corruptible things, *as* silver and gold, from your vain conversation *received* by tradition from your fathers; But with the precious blood of Christ, as of a lamb without blemish and without spot: Who verily was foreordained before the foundation of the world, but was manifest in these last times for you, (1 Peter 1:18-20).

The content of the gospel or the good news is simple: it is the fact that the original problem of sin has been solved by God through Christ's precious blood. It has to be Christ's precious blood because it is a sinless blood that can atone for man's sin according to God's law and justice - (Hebrews 9:22). In a nutshell, the good news is that although sin separated man from his Maker, his true Essence and Power, Christ the Redeemer has prevailed over sin and paid the price in full. "To the praise of the glory of his grace, wherein he hath made us accepted in

<u>the beloved.</u>" (Ephesians 1:6)

Consequently, man has now been saved, redeemed and can be fully restored to God's power grid without let or hindrance. However, there has to be a proof or certificate of discharge that a man has been redeemed and restored to God's power grid. This proof is the Holy Spirit.

The most important evidence of man's freedom or redemption from sin is God's seal of approval called the Holy Spirit. This is why the Bible tells us not to be ashamed of the gospel of Christ because, "it is <u>the power of God unto salvation</u>" – Romans 1:16.

Every man is ruled by a spirit. The natural man is ruled by a strange spirit of unbelief, wickedness, depravity and pride – the Bible calls it "the spirit that now works in the children of disobedience - (Ephesians 2:2). Satan, by nature, loves to keep men in the bondage of sin forever; consequently, *he does not* ever *open the house of his prisoners* according to Isaiah 14:17, except he is overpowered.

The Lord once warned His disciples in the book of Matthew 12:29 and Mark 3:27 that it is suicidal to walk casually into a strong man's house and take his goods without first of all binding him.

This means that salvation itself cannot just occur without divine intervention. Satan is not that friendly. Even after receiving the good news, a natural man needs

God's special grace before he can see it for what it truly is or embrace it as he should. This explains why the gospel is not just another mere news or regular history that the natural man can unravel. It is not cunningly devised fables or motivational speaking; it is a power packed information that sets free!

> And ye shall know the truth, and the truth shall make you free. (John 8:32)

> And I, brethren, when I came to you, came not with excellency of speech or of wisdom, declaring unto you the testimony of God. And my speech and my preaching was not with enticing words of man's wisdom, but in demonstration of the Spirit and of power: That your faith should not stand in the wisdom of men, but in the power of God. 1 Corinthians 2:1, 4,5.

Any faith that is born out of men's reasoning is devoid of God's power. No man can help God when it comes to the salvation of the soul of men.

This explains why we must be careful with extra biblical ideologies in our evangelistic efforts. God is the one that births faith in the unbeliever, or else, he isn't born of God but of the will of man. Salvation is God's power at work through His Holy Spirit poured out upon men. Any salvation that occurs, devoid of this power is fake. It will not last for long. One of the infallible pieces of evidence that a person has been saved by God's own power is that s/he is also endued with power from on High. If not, the work is incomplete. Salvation requires the element of power and the purpose of the power element is to,

a.  convict sinners (Satan's captives);
b.  disarm Satan;
c.  free his captives;
d.  justify and glorify the freed, i.e., turn them into new creatures;
e.  equip, embolden and empower them for witnessing;
f.  and seal or sanctify and preserve them from sin or the corruption that is in the world through lust and its eternal consequences.

The different stages of the power and work of the Holy Spirit in bringing about the total package of redemption among men is here illustrated.

> And we know that all things work together for good to them that love God, to them who are the called according to *his* purpose. For whom he did foreknow, he also did predestinate *to be* conformed to the image of his Son, that he might be the firstborn among many brethren. Moreover whom he did predestinate, them he also called: and whom he called, them he also justified: and whom he justified, them he also glorified. (Romans 8:28-30)

Two levels of the same power are here referred to and released through God's Holy Spirit at salvation:

> In whom ye also trusted, after that ye heard the word of truth, the gospel of your salvation… (Ephesians 1:13a)

## 1. The Power of God unto Salvation (Baptism into Christ) –

This is the power of the Holy Spirit poured out to begin or activate the work of salvation in sinful men. It starts by bringing men under the conviction of sin and opens their eyes to the need for the Saviour. The Holy Spirit basically shows a man his true condition. It is as if a wretched man in his squalor meets a stinking rich man in all his glory. He needs no further convincing or arguments to know that he is wretched because he can literally see a sharp contrast with his wretchedness right before him. This is what humbles the sinner and weighs heavily on his heart so much so that he sees an urgent need to repent – 2Corinthians 7:10. It is as good as a scale falling off a blind man's eyes and he is able to see for the first time his pitiable condition of wretchedness. It is the power that opens the gate of hell and death and allows a man to walk away from it without further delay or hindrance. Here, the chains of sin and Satan are broken and "the new birth" happens. Here, God's purchasing power or redemptive power, if you please, is activated to bring the sinner in contact with the full implication of Christ's atoning death on Calvary. At this point, he hears his Maker saying to him, your debts are "paid in full"; go and sin no more". This event is so powerful that it results in total deliverance and releases men from the consequences of their past sins, its guilt and consequences.

The Holy Spirit convicts men *of sin, and of righteousness, and of judgment.* This is the first half of His work on earth. Christ's work is both physical and spiritual because He mediates between the physical man and the spiritual God, when the Holy Spirit is released. However, it is a reunion of the physical man with the Spirit and power of the unseen but known God. It is like the consummation of the new union. Jesus paid the price, while the Holy Spirit convicts of sin, and leads men to repentance. He also seals and preserves men until the day of redemption. Without the Holy Spirit's power, knowing the truth, accepting it and repentance is practically impossible. This is the first work the Spirit of God does in a man.

**Enduement with Power from on High (Baptism of the Holy Spirit)** – This is the same Spirit's power that saves, (i.e., the same Spirit of faith – 2Corinthians 4:13), but there is more after the initial work of salvation,

> ...in whom <u>also after that ye believed, ye were sealed</u> with that holy Spirit of promise, Which is the earnest of our inheritance until the redemption of the purchased possession, unto the praise of his glory. (Ephesians 1:13-14)

Many today are oblivious of the fact that being born again is the beginning, and there is more. It is possible to be a weak, vulnerable and powerless Christian. A Christian who is not baptized in the Holy Spirit (with or without the evidence of tongues) is missing a great deal of God's power; he can be easily manipulated by Satan and be entangled again with the yoke of bondage – Galatians 5:1. Without being endued with power, a believer will mostly remain weak in faith, s/he will be neither cold nor warm, s/he will not be an effective witness of the cross of Christ and s/he will be carnal and not spiritual. To be spiritual is to be Spirit filled; there are no two ways about it!

> And I, brethren, could not speak unto you as unto spiritual, but as unto carnal, *even* as unto babes in Christ. I have fed you with milk, and not with meat: for hitherto ye were not able *to bear it,* neither yet now are ye able. For ye are yet carnal: for whereas *there is* among you envying, and strife, and divisions, are ye not carnal, and walk as men? (1 Corinthians 3:1)

This is why we must all answer this all-important question in the affirmative if we are to grow in the faith and be victorious over sin and Satan, "…have ye received the Holy Ghost since ye believed?" (Acts 19:2a). The Holy Spirit upon and within the believer is God's grace; yea, His raw power poured out upon the weak. He is poured out upon saved mortals to keep them saved, able and stable, come what may. It is the Spirit that *quickens* the believer to live his *new life* through Christ or live out the life of Christ – i.e., a life of love. The Holy Spirit is called or described with many appellations in the Bible. Let's examine these two:

1.        *Treasure in earthen vessels* - 2 Corinthians 4:7. As God's Spirit dwells in, rests upon and resides in man, He quickens him now and will yet quicken him at the resurrection - *But if the Spirit of him that raised up Jesus from the dead dwell in you, he that raised up Christ from the dead shall also quicken your mortal bodies by his Spirit that dwelleth in you.* (Romans 8:11). In a manner of speaking, He is *resident power* as against the old condition or state of *resident evil.* Remember, without the Holy Spirit, ...in me (that is, in my flesh,) dwelleth no good thing: for to will is present with me; but how to perform that which is good I find not. (Romans 7:18). He is the one who remedies this situation. Without the Holy Spirit, a person is as good as a sinner. *But ye are not in the flesh, but in the Spirit, if so be that the Spirit of God dwell in you. Now <u>if any man have not the Spirit of Christ, he is none of his.</u>* - (Romans 8:9)

God in His infinite wisdom pours out His Spirit upon saved men to differentiate them from those who are still being led by the spirit of this world – His Spirit is His identification mark upon the saved. *But we have this <u>treasure in earthen vessels,</u> that the <u>excellency of the power</u> <u>may be</u> <u>of God, and not of us.</u>*

If this Treasure is missing, a man has not received power, even if he claims to be a believer. The Spirit upon and within is God's mark of excellence, or His quality assurance seal, if you please. This explains why only those with this seal are capable of displaying *the excellency of power* which when rated, examined or assessed, can only be derived from God. When exercised, love is always on display and its attending glory goes back to God because, ultimately, the fruit of the Spirit is love.

> But the fruit of the Spirit is love, joy, peace, longsuffering, gentleness, goodness, faith, Meekness, temperance: against such there is no law. And they that are Christ's have crucified the flesh with the affections and lusts. (Galatians 5:2-24)

2.	*The trademark or Seal of God upon/within a man* — A trademark is a symbol or a recognisable sign, design or insignia which identifies products or services of a particular source from those of others. Trademarks are usually distinctive or unique; they reveal or show ownership or identity.

Everyone who truly accepts Christ is then granted the upper room experience – they are baptised in the Holy Ghost as a mark that they are now a member of God's family. The real trademark of believers transcends joining a church, praying and fasting, attending special church programmes, becoming a worker in the Church, singing in the choir or attending a bible college; it is power! *"For the kingdom of God is not in word, but in power"* *1 Corinthians 4:20*. Anyone can speak, sing, talk and motivate others; there are natural orators and excellent communicators. This explains why other religions, devoid of power, can also sound good and command a sizable number of followers and devotees. Unfortunately, a person who accepts religion without God's power can only display *a form of godliness devoid of power* that should sustain it because another word for powerless love is …*Having a form of godliness, but denying the power thereof...* (2 Timothy 3:5). The bible warns that we should *"from such turn away."*

Let me reiterate this: there is a limit to which the arm of flesh can take a person before it *breaks down* in love. This is the truth. There is yet a depth of love and a height of which the arm of flesh does not know and *cannot* climb. This explains why people break down on love journeys, and sometimes they break down irreparably. That's when you start hearing statements like: "I am no longer in love with him/her" or "we have irreconcilable differences; therefore, we must go our separate ways" or "I have fallen for someone else." These are most times nothing but tell-tale signs that a person's love engine has run out of power, fuel or steam. He has disconnected from the Spirit of love. Except God's Spirit breathes on such an individual, the damage is usually permanent.

Now you know why a man could be on fire one moment and become totally weary, worn out and discouraged the next minute. Be not surprised my friend, …*It is the Spirit that quickeneth; the flesh profiteth nothing…* John 6: 63. Love is *quickened*, it is not to be expected from man's undulating emotions.

Christ did not only die to redeem our dead spirits; He went further to seal us with His Holy Spirit so that Satan will never be able to take us down like He did Adam.

> In whom ye also trusted, after that ye heard the word of truth, the gospel of your salvation: in whom also after that ye believed, ye were _sealed with that holy Spirit of promise_ – (Ephesians 1:13)

We have been sealed by the Holy Spirit. That is our trademark; that is God's mark of ownership and protection upon all who come to Him through Christ. As long as we remain plugged to Him, we will always produce love; it is automatic

> (For the fruit of the Spirit is in all goodness and righteousness and truth;) Proving what is acceptable unto the Lord – Ephesians 5:9-10.

This is why the Lord insisted that no one could bear fruit that is outside or separate from the Vine.

> I am the vine, ye are the branches: He that abideth in me, and I in him, the same bringeth forth much fruit: for without me

ye can do nothing. John 15:5

Disconnecting from the vine equals to being vulnerable. It makes men casualties, and amplifies our weaknesses. In this state, we can do *nothing* in the face of Satan's assaults. This is the state when we find out that we cannot carry on *loving* because we are detached from the Tree of love and like a wise saying *among the Yorubas, "a stream that forgets its source will dry up"*.

In all, if a person's *love lines* or *fair speeches* and *good intentions* are devoid of God's power, it doesnot always produce a good outcome.

Consequently, contrary to the notion that love leads to untoward behaviours, including, fleshly lusts, debauchery, inordinate affection, fornication, adultery, uncleanness, lasciviousness, etc., the opposite is what is obtainable in love. Love is therefore not the reason behind that overpowering feeling that leads to insolence, uncleanness and sinfulness. Instead, love is a fruit of the Holy Spirit characterised by joy, peace, longsuffering, gentleness, faith, meekness, and temperance in men.

Finally, note the word *Holy* that precedes the word *Spirit*. What this means is that the real name of the Spirit we are saved by, baptised and sealed with is *HOLY*. The spirit aspect was added to let us know that He is not human or flesh and blood. His name is Holy!

And one cried unto another, and said, Holy,

> holy, holy, is the LORD of hosts: the whole earth is full of his glory. (Isaiah 6:3)
> And the four beasts had each of them six wings about him; and they were full of eyes within: and they rest not day and night, saying, Holy, holy, holy, Lord God Almighty, which was, and is, and is to come. (Revelation 4:8)

Consequently, holiness is one of the unmistakable signs of Love. If love is devoid of holiness, it is not the true and unfailing love of God. This is why God permits everyone who claims to have met Him and is living according to the Spirit to be subjected to a set of standardised tests. If the love you claim to have is true or false, God's standardised testing is the way to know. In book two, the issue of test and its importance is further examined. Get your copy today and find out more about Love Ramifications!

Thanks for your time.

God bless you!

## Chapter Precepts

1.  The Godhead is made of the Father God Almighty, The Word is Christ and the Holy Ghost is His Spirit. All three are equal, according to the scriptures

2.  Without Christ, the Holy Ghost wouldn't have come and without the Holy Ghost, no man can bear the fruit of love. Christ is the baptizer with the Holy Spirit

3.  The Fruit of The Spirit is Love. This means that until we are engrafted into the tree of love, bearing the fruit of love remains a mere wish; it is impossible!

4.  contrary to the notion that love leads to untoward behaviours, including, fleshly lusts, debauchery, inordinate affection, fornication, adultery, uncleanness, lasciviousness, etc., the opposite is what is obtainable in love. Love is therefore not the reason behind that overpowering feeling that leads to insolence, uncleanness and sinfulness. Instead, love is a fruit of the Holy Spirit characterised by joy, peace, longsuffering, gentleness, faith, meekness, and

temperance in men.

5.  His name is Holy! Consequently, holiness is one of the unmistakeable signs of Love.

6.  If love is devoid of holiness, it is not the true and unfailing love of God.

Anticipate...
THIS JULY
THE POWER OF LOVE SERIES
BOOK ONE
IS THIS LOVE I AM FEELING?
AN INTRODUCTION TO LOVE
TUNDE IDOWU-TAYLOR
THE POWER OF LOVE SERIES
BOOK TWO
LOVE RAMI-FICATIONS
LOVING GOD, LOVING SELF & LOVING OTHERS
TUNDE IDOWU-TAYLOR
IDOWU-TAYLOR
IS THIS LOVE I AM FEELING?

Join me on
The BIBLE STUDY CHANNEL
IN-DEPTH. INCISIVE. PRACTICAL.
Holy Spirit inspired & Life Transforming
LIVE & PRE-RECORDED
TEXT, AUDIO & VIDEO FORMATS
...Rightly dividing the word of truth

SINGLE | SEARCHING | COURTING | MARRIED | ABOUT TO WED
Listen, Download & Share the
Ladies Gist with PREYE
A journey of discovery for godly women
PODCAST
OYINPREYE IDOWU-TAYLOR
FINDING TRUE LOVE Series
NEW EPISODE EVERY SUNDAY
https://ladiesgistwithpreye.podomatic.com/
Follow Ladies Gist with Preye on
A journey of discovery for godly women...
08062655862

CELEBRATING ELEVEN YEARS OF Tangible Impact
THIRD EDITION
2010
FIRST EDITION
2021
2016
SECOND EDITION
A FAITHFUL MAN YOU CAN FIND!
TUNDE IDOWU-TAYLOR
TUNDE IDOWU-TAYLOR
Buy the truth, and sell it not; also wisdom, and instruction, and understanding.
- (Proverbs 23:23)
★ 11 YEARS ★
3RD EDITION
ANNIVERSARY
Available now at
BrookStones Stores
8, VICTORIA COURT, MINT ESTATE
BY LAGOS BUSINESS SCHOOL, LEKKI-AJAH, LAGOS
08035630958; 08062655862
SAME DAY DELIVERY SERVICE
AVAILABLE ACROSS LAGOS
amazon

A Call to Biblical Christianity
GIVE
ATTENTION
TO
DOCTRINE
TUNDE IDOWU TAYLOR
Introducing...
GIVE ATTENTION TO
DOCTRINE
A Call to Biblical Christianity
PAPERBACK
Buy the truth, and sell it not;
also wisdom, and instruction,
and understanding. (Proverbs 23:23)
AVAILABLE NOW AT
amazon
NairaTree store
AFFORDABLE LUXURY AT YOUR DOORSTEP
5, FATAI OLUSESI STR.,
BY LEKKI CONSERVATION CENTRE
OPPOSITE CHEVRON, LEKKI LAGOS NIGERIA
08035630958, 08062655862
NATIONWIDE DELIVERY
SAME DAY DELIVERY SERVICE
AVAILABLE ACROSS LAGOS

TÜNDE & PREYE IDOWU-TAYLOR
MERRY CHRISTMAS
Wish you
the happiest
holidays
FRUITFUL PEOPLE

LIVING FOR GOD
A Counterculture Revolution
IDOWU-TAYLOR
Atlans Publishing HOUSE
Theology is the doctrine or teaching of living for God though Christ, by the Spirit, in the context of the church, and with a view to the glories of heaven - Mark Jones
Available now at
NairaTree Store
5, FATAI OLUSESI STR.,
BY LEKKI CONSERVATION CENTRE
OPPOSITE CHEVRON; LEKKI LAGOS NIGERIA
08035630958; 08062655862
SAME DAY DELIVERY SERVICE
AVAILABLE ACROSS LAGOS
Also available on amazon.com

Revised +
Updated
Newly Published!
"Buy the truth, and sell it not;
Also wisdom and instruction and
understanding." Proverbs 23:23
THE
POWER
OF
PURITY
Let your garments be always white...
TUNDE IDOWU-TAYLOR
Foreword by Rev. Victor Odunjo
Let your garments be always white... Eccl. 9:8
amazon
Available at
amazon
& amazonkindle

And that he died for all, that they which live should not henceforth live unto themselves, but unto him which died for them, and rose again.

– 2CORINTHIANS 5:15




LIVING FOR GOD
A COUNTERCULTURE REVOLUTION
PAPERBACK

AVAILABLE NOW ON
NairaTree Stores
AFFORDABLE LIBRARY AT YOUR DOORSTEP

TUNDE IDOWU-TAYLOR

5, FATAI OLUSESI STR.,
BY LEKKI CONSERVATION CENTRE
OPPOSITE CHEVRON, LEKKI LAGOS NIGERIA

NATIONWIDE DELIVERY

SAME DAY DELIVERY SERVICE
AVAILABLE ACROSS LAGOS

07038678269      NAIRATREE STORES


Buy the truth, and sell it not; also wisdom, and instruction, and understanding. (Proverbs 23:23)

www.ingramcontent.com/pod-product-compliance
Lightning Source LLC
Chambersburg PA
CBHW070516160726
48003CB00004B/1587